PARTY
INGREDIENTS

PARTY INGREDIENTS

CREATIVE MENUS AND IDEAS
FOR EVERY ENTERTAINING OCCASION

PETER GLADWIN

CASSELL

To Susie Robinson who taught me to cook and without whom the first 'Party Ingredients' would never have started

A CASSELL BOOK

First published in the UK 1994
by Cassell
Villiers House
41/47 Strand
London
WC2N 5JE

Photography by Nadia Mackenzie
Food for photography by Peter Gladwin and Olivia Stewart-Cox

Distributed in the United States
by Sterling Publishing Co, Inc.
387 Park Avenue South, New York,
New York 10016-8810

Distributed in Australia
by Capricorn Link (Australia) Pty Ltd
2/13 Carrington Road, Castle Hill, NSW 2154

British Library Cataloguing-in-Publication Data
A catalogue record for this book is available from the British Library

ISBN 0-304-34341-2

Typeset by Method Limited, Epping, Essex, UK

Printed and bound in Great Britain by
Hollen Street Press Limited

Contents

Introduction

Haven't you had enough of long-winded, technical recipes that make you feel inadequate and leave you a slave in the kitchen when you could be having fun with your guests? I certainly have. Indeed, I have spent my whole working life finding ways of creating inspired food that's practical to cook and serve when entertaining, and I am not ashamed of it. If you are one of those purist cordon whatsits, you are going to hate me – an instant stock cube here, a shortcut there, some blatant contradictions of fine cooking principles but if the results taste and look delicious, who cares!

This book is a collection of different party suggestions and recipes for each season of the year. Some are frivolous, some more formal, but all of them are dedicated to you enjoying your own parties. Please use the recipes either individually or in conjunction with ideas of your own and take or leave my cryptic advice as you wish.

Whether we are cooking for four or forty, let's give imaginative stylish parties and be relaxed and stress-free to entertain our guests. I hope!

Happy entertaining.

Planning a Party

There are only two really good reasons for giving a party: either you have something to celebrate or you just feel like celebrating something. Both are equally worthwhile but then there are also all those other occasions when duty calls – the boss and his wife to dinner, or 'they did invite us'. Whatever the reason and whether it's to be a small supper party or a buffet for 30, you want to do your best. Good advance planning is the key to success. Here is a simple checklist of everything you need to think about.

- The occasion?
- What form should the party take: a coke and crisps or a seven-course banquet?
- Style of food – stand up, sit down, even lie down?
- Themes, music and entertainment
- Date, timing and invitations
- Number of guests and who to invite?
- Menu planning, shopping lists and shopping
- Cooking in advance: when will you prepare?
- Layout, extra chairs or tables – can you borrow the neighbours' without inviting them?!
- Plates, knives, forks, napkins and so on
- Drinks, ice and glasses
- Flowers and decorations
- Setting up and table-laying – and on certain occasions, removing precious objects
- Change, have a drink and relax before your guests arrive!

Some of these headings are self-explanatory and some I have developed on the following pages.

THEMES AND ENTERTAINMENT

A word of caution here. Of course a successful theme party or outrageous entertainment can be fun. But equally I have seen many such parties where it does not quite come off – half the guests dressed in togas and the others in evening dress, both groups rather uncomfortable, lacking the Roman decadence to match the theme. Or what I call a 'lead balloon stripagram', grossly embarrassing the 'birthday boy' and guests alike with an indecent assault on his dignity.

For themes and entertainments it is vital that you consider the tastes of your guests as well as your own. What may seem screamingly funny when discussed *à deux* in the bath may not be nearly as light-hearted when the Chairman's wife actually arrives. Plan the party for everyone's pleasure and if a good theme can add to the enjoyment, then that's great.

Choosing a theme The simpler the theme, the easier it will be for everyone to join in. Colours are most effective – black, silver, white, green, red – you choose; the food, drinks, dress and decorations can then all be tied in.

Let's take *red* as an example. You will surely send red invitations and stipulate 'something red' as the required dress. Your guests' interpretation of this will range from a cautious red carnation to a Chinese flag with a hole cut in the middle to fit like a kaftan. Your home can be draped in red crêpe paper with the odd 'keep left' sign to amuse the more politically minded. Investment will be needed in a large bottle of red food colouring (think of those dreadful E numbers!) and then a suitably dyed Chicken Tandoori may be served, followed by red fruit salad. A welcome drink of lurid red Buck's Fizz made from cartons of blood red orange juice and then, thank goodness, we can all enjoy a civilized glass of red wine.

This leads us on to the classic theme of 'fancy dress'. Will your guests be willing to 'play' and will they be able to find something suitable? The problem with historic themes is that although *you* may have a complete Louis XIV outfit languishing in a cupboard, not everyone does, nor do we all want to go out and hire one. Themes like infamous politicians, Elvis and Madonna, Hollywood stars, tarts and vicars are easier to be inventive with.

It is a mistake to think that theme parties automatically imply dressing up. The theme can also be an activity – a croquet party, a gambling party, a murder, or good old rock and roll. Rock and roll will inevitably inspire those who could never quite bring themselves to part with that pair of winklepickers. Catering is easy too – 'dogs' with onions, ketchup and bottles of 'Bud' will be ideal.

Food themes in general can be great fun although they do put the pressure on the cook. As long as you enjoy a day in the kitchen, then a selection of Chinese, Russian or New Orleans dishes, for instance, will make a great original meal. Music, entertainment and dress can be added to suit.

Musical entertainments

It is wonderful to have music at a party – celebrating with feasting and dancing has always gone hand in hand and there are all sorts of options for you to consider. From a philharmonic orchestra to a steel band, musicians the world over are eager to perform and give of their best. Let's not get too carried away though – budget and the size of your living room may be restrictions here, so what about a music student playing the flute after dinner?

Discotheques can be excellent as long as the disc jockey is entertaining the audience rather than himself (this may require a little guidance from the hosts). Alternatively, good quality records and tapes will be perfect if you take the trouble to plan what is to be played in advance.

Finally, let me get my grouch in against 'background music' – that's that wonderful discreet stereo which you cannot actually hear, but nonetheless conversation has to battle against. If music is to be enjoyed, let's have it loud in the dancing area and quiet where people may want to have an opportunity to talk.

Other entertainments

I cannot begin to list all the other entertainments which are available to enliven your parties. From a rowdy session of 'at home karaoke' to good old-fashioned charades, each can be great fun in the right circumstances. Do you want to make a witty speech, invent a word quiz or listen to a stand-up comedian? Perhaps we'll just settle for a game of Scrabble.

INVITATIONS

Your invitation can be a casual phone call or a gilt-edged embossed card. Just ensure that all the Ws are included: **Who**, **Where**, **When**, **Why** and **What**. The 'What' is most commonly forgotten – what sort of party it is and what's on offer. For example, if you say 'drinks' and then provide supper, you will be disappointed when half your guests have taken the precaution of eating before they arrive. Or if your guests turn up dressed for swimming and you planned opera, they may feel a little awkward.

Such examples could get sillier and sillier so I will stop but I am sure you have got the idea.

Impromptu invitations

I think it is up to the individual whether to invite guests well in advance and have lots of preparation time or whether to say 'come and have supper tonight'. I enjoy doing both – it is very satisfying to work towards a party but, equally, an impromptu invitation carries no expectations for the guests and a very simple occasion can be great fun.

The half-way compromise of planning in advance but resisting inviting your guests until the last minute in the hope that your evening will feel impromptu is definitely a

11

recipe for disaster – your guests will not be available, your planning will be blatantly obvious and you will just be disappointed with the result.

Surprise   Now the big question – is a surprise party going to be just great fun for the 'thrower' or will the recipient actually enjoy it too? If you are quite certain it will go down well, you need carefully planned tactics for keeping the victim out of the way and discreet guests who will arrive on time. Why not try a surprise party for two – less shock and more romance!

Menu Planning

I have already promised to help you make the cooking side of things as easy as possible, but that is not to say you shouldn't enjoy planning and preparing the 'do'. On the contrary you have the chance to show off all that flair and skill you hardly knew you had!

When planning your menus there are five criteria I would recommend:

Seasonal   Use ingredients and recipes to suit the time of year. You will see that this book is divided into the four seasons of the year.

Visual   Your food needs to look as delicious as it tastes, so please wipe away the drips and don't skimp on the decoration.

Balanced   I have presented a lot of my recipes as complete menu suggestions. Do swap these around but avoid serving too much pastry in a meal, too many rich dishes or repetitive colours and shapes.

Consider your guests   Watch out for vegetarians, religious dietary restrictions or other diets for that matter. It's not always possible to know and a spare avocado in stock can sometimes save a lot of embarrassment!

And be imaginative Be a little bit adventurous – at worst it will be a disaster! I hope some of the ideas I have suggested will help you to develop others of your own.

Cooking in Advance

If at all possible, you should allocate some time well before your guests arrive to prepare everything. You will then feel confident that you are in control of the meal.

This is not the same thing as cooking the whole meal beforehand and leaving it stewing in a warming cupboard – some last minute action is vital to producing good food. You will see, however, that I have divided most recipes for hot dishes into 'preparation' and 'final cooking and serving'. This is a great habit to get into – all the complicated bits are done beforehand and you only need to remain sober enough to put things in, or more importantly remember to take things out of the oven at the right time.

Party Booze

I am glad to say that we all eventually grow out of the teenage philosophy which says 'get everyone paralytic and they are bound to have a good time'. All the same, drinks at a party are important and in my view need to be plentiful, delectable, limited in choice, but both alcoholic and soft. Too many choices of drinks can confuse guests and make refilling glasses a difficult job for the hosts. Not everyone wants to drink vast quantities of alcohol and something delicious but 'soft' may well be a popular option.

There is nothing worse than waiting and hoping to be offered another drink. Oh yes there is – when you are presented with that 'special cocktail' which is so undrinkable you dread being offered another one.

Even if your friends tend to bring a bottle with them, I suggest you still invest in sufficient wine for the whole party. That way your drinks will all be suitably chilled (or not) and consistent. Treat the bottles brought as a present for your 'cellar' – in the long run they should save you buying wines for weeks to come and therefore not cost you any more. Just be careful you don't take the same bottle back to those who brought it. They may think you did not like their choice!

Specials   Having made derogatory remarks about 'special cocktails', I hate to think how many of my friends will now have taken great offence on the assumption that theirs was the one. In principle, however, I am a great believer in offering a special welcoming drink as long as it is not intended to 'set you up for the night'. Guffaw! and it should actually taste nice. The classics like Kir made with white wine and cassis or Pimms No 1 or even a good mulled wine are all lovely welcoming drinks.

Quantities   It is difficult for me to advise on exactly how much your friends will drink; their age group, the weather, occasion and duration will all be factors. However, the accepted quantities to allow are detailed below. The heavy drinkers and the abstainers will average one another out. It's much better to have too much than to be stingy and do not forget my reminder about soft drinks including mineral water – you really should not run out of these.

Drinks parties   ½ bottle of wine per person or equivalent

Lunchtimes and Buffets   1½ drinks before and ½ bottle of wine

Dinner parties   2 drinks before and ⅔ bottle of wine thereafter

Preparing   A little time spent preparing your drinks is always worthwhile. The cheapest and most uninteresting white wine will be infinitely nicer served ice-cold from the refrigerator in an attractive polished glass. Any red wine, too, will benefit from warming to room temperature, opening well in advance and even decanting. Gin needs ice and lemon, Martinis need olives and so on.

Choosing Finally, I would like to offer you some ideas on choosing the drinks for your parties. As the owner of an English vineyard I naturally recommend my own crisp, dry English white wine for practically every occasion, but in case you occasionally want to stray from this valuable advice, I have given below some other suggestions for you to consider.

Drinks parties Sparklers from France, Germany, Spain or Australia
Tasty whites: Australian Chardonnays, Alsace or Sancerre
Lightish reds: Valpolicella, Brouilly or Fleurie
Pimms No 1, punches, cups or cocktails

Buffets – wines for quaffing Whites: Orvieto, New Zealand, Sauvignon, Hungarian Pinot
Reds: southern French, Chilean Merlot, Tuscan

Sunny salads and picnics Elderflower Champagne or Pimms No 1
Whites: Vinho Verde, English Bacchus, Bordeaux dry
Reds: Beaujolais, Loire or southern French rosé

Brunch Gallons of black coffee
Bloody Mary or Champagne

Lunch or simple suppers Whites: English dry, Rieslings or light Italians
Reds: Bulgarian Cabernet Sauvignon, Australian Shiraz or Chianti

Barbecues Strong Whites: Rioja, Californian Chardonnay or Gewürztraminer
Big Reds: Rhône, Rioja or Australian Cabernet Sauvignon

Indian or Chinese Quantities of lager or light inexpensive white wines such as Soave, Frascati, Chardonnays

Dinner parties   Here the sky is the limit and I can only really guide you on what style of wine goes with different dishes:
Salads or seafood   Whites: Moselle, English Schönburger, Frascati or Muscadet
Soups   dry sherries, Gewürztraminer and Spanish whites
Fish dishes   Whites: Pouilly-Fumé, white Burgundy or New Zealand Chardonnay
White meats or vegetarian main courses   Whites: full-bodied Californian or Australian Chardonnay, fine white Burgundy
Reds: Pinot Noir, Tuscan reds or lighter claret
Red meats or game   Reds: big Rhône wines, red Burgundys, Bordeaux, Barolo, Rioja or Australian Shiraz Cabernet
Cheese courses   Châteauneuf-du-Pape, a good claret or port
Fruity puddings   Champagne, New World Late Harvest or English Huzelrebe
Gooey puddings   Sauternes, Muscat and Auslese

Christmas Day   Sweet sherry for Gran, claret for Uncle Albert, champagne for the Mrs and beer for the rest – perfect.

FLOWERS, DECORATIONS AND LIGHTING

Flowers   At the risk of damaging my port-swigging, Stilton-guzzling, macho image forever, I have to say how much I love flowers at a party. Just a jar of daisies on a supper table will make all the difference. You will probably find a lot of what is needed in your garden and it's no use saying you are hopeless at arranging flowers. Simplicity is the key: a huge jug of spring daffodils, bold country blooms stuffed in a vase just as you feel, an urn of autumn leaves, or a basket of fir cones and holly.

If you find cut flowers last too short a time, then use potted plants: a matching set of white and deep mauve hydrangeas in terracotta pots, or the rich red of poinsettias overflowing an old coal scuttle.

Wonderful contrasting shades of foliage can also be used as a natural base for buffet food or to fill a dreary corner.

Decoration

Decorations for a party cover everything from Christmas streamers to the choice of tablecloths and napkins. Some sort of colour co-ordination or contrast works well – for example, using raspberry pink napkins on a deep blue tablecloth with a cluster of blue and pink balloons as the table centrepiece. Balloon decorating has become an art in itself for some parties, although I do feel they are an alternative rather than a complement to flowers.

Lighting

Lighting for evening parties should also be considered part of the decoration. Gloom is not attractive and the secret is not to simply turn lights down until no one can see the plate in front of them. Candlelight is lovely but you usually need some discreet background lighting as well. Lastly, if you are entertaining out of doors, don't forget that it gets dark. That may sound like stating the obvious but it's easily forgotten on a balmy summer's night and you only realize that the light has gone when the blackened food on the barbecue has become invisible.

Decorating food

How many times have I heard – 'It's those finishing touches which make all the difference,' and yet how often is the sprinkling of parsley or sprig of watercress forgotten at the last moment?

That awful word 'garnish' conjures up twists of orange and maraschino cherries slotted on to the side of prawn cocktails and banana splits alike. Heaven forbid that is what we are after, but a little gentle decorating really will make all the difference: a single rose petal on top of an ice-cream, a maple leaf tucked under the base of a ramekin, sprigs of fresh herbs or fanned slices of fruits. The decoration should relate to the food, either high-lighting certain ingredients or visually complementing the colour or shape. All I ask is that the food looks as lovely as the hostess!

Dinner Party Technique

Throughout this book I go on about relaxing at your own dinner party but at the same time serving stunning food. Perhaps you feel this is easier said than done? How can you avoid jumping up from the table every three minutes to poke at the bullet-hard potatoes in the hope they might one day be cooked?

Once again the answers are easy – good preparation and pre-cooking will give you the necessary confidence to relax. If you know that your starters are ready on the side, the sauce just needs heating up, your vegetables are cooked to perfection and will only need warming through, and the *pièce de resistance* birthday pud just awaits the candles to be lit, then that gin and tonic slips down and you really do start to enjoy yourself – I promise. Here is a summary of tips to help you to perfect your dinner party technique:

Table laying	Think through each course you are going to serve – plates, cutlery, serving spoons and dishes, mats, etc.
Wines and drinks	Glasses ready? Are the wines chilled or warmed and opened ready to serve? Soft drinks, ice and dare I say a corkscrew?
Cold starters and cold puddings	Most of these can be completely prepared, arranged on plates and ready to serve, covered in cling film and left in a cool place. The exceptions are dressings and sauces, which can be prepared in advance but should only be added at the very last minute.
Hot starters	Prepared completely in advance but most should be cooked just before serving.

Soups	Made beforehand and reheated just before serving.
Roast meats	With the exception of fillet of beef, roast meats should finish cooking before dinner begins and then be kept warm 'resting' for 30 minutes before carving and serving.
Fish main courses	Can be prepared in advance but must be cooked just before serving.
Other main courses	Prepared in advance, then final cooking or reheating while the starter is being eaten.
Roux-based sauces	Made in advance and reheated when needed. Meat juices can always be added at the end.
Butter-based sauces	Prepared in advance, then carefully warmed in a bowl over hot water.
Sauces thickened with egg yolks and cream or arrowroot	The base liquid can be prepared but thickening must be done at the last minute.
Vegetables cooked in advance	Plunged into boiling water and cooked until tender but still crisp. Drained and immediately chilled under cold water. Just before serving the minimum reheating is required by *one* of the following methods: ● tossing in a covered pan with some butter for 2–4 minutes ● plunging back into boiling water for 1–2 minutes ● placing in a hot oven in a covered dish with a little butter for 5–10 minutes.
Roast vegetables	Roasted and kept hot – don't attempt reheating.
Hot puddings	Most of these can be cooked beforehand and then warmed through during a pause after the main course is finished.
Coffee and Chocolates	I know I am repeating myself but again – cups, saucers, spoons, sugar, cream and coffee all at the ready. Did the guests bring the chocs?

Cooking for Large Numbers

At one extreme there is the anxious host or hostess wielding a tiny ladle in the fear that the food is about to run out and at the other, guests are subjected to desperate pressure to eat more because no impression has been made on the mountain of food provided, although everyone has had their fill. How do you get it right? To begin with, we must dispel the myth that cooking for thirty is an entirely different animal to cooking for six. Obviously more food will be required for more people and the preparation will take longer but both the principles of cooking and the amount each individual eats remain the same.

Quantities The party recipes I have included in this book are mainly for six people. For double the numbers, just double the quantities. For certain dishes, however, it may be preferable to make the recipe two or three times rather than just multiply the quantities. This especially applies to meringues, mousses and soufflés, or dishes requiring frying or sautéeing. The size of your saucepans and cooker will help to dictate this.

It gets more complicated when you wish to offer a choice or put your own buffet menus together. Inevitably, faced with a choice, lots of people plump for some of each (it saves their making a decision) – you must therefore make sure your portions can be easily divided and that you allow extra in case one dish is more popular than another. It is also nice to be able to offer second helpings. The following are details of the quantities I would recommend:

| *Dinner parties for 12 people* | Choice of two starters | 8 portions of each |
| | Choice of main course | Chaos in the kitchen – not to be recommended |

	Choice of two puddings	12 portions of the one you consider best; 6 portions of the other
	Choice of three puddings	6 portions of each
Vegetables	Potatoes	Prepared weight: 150–175g/5–6oz per person
	Other vegetables	Choice of two, prepared weight: 75g/3oz of each per person
	Vegetable medley	150g/5oz per person overall
Buffets for 12 people	Choice of two main courses	10 portions of the one you consider best; 8 portions of the other
	Choice of three main courses	6 portions of each
	Choice of three salads	6 portions of each
	Choice of two puddings	12 portions of the one you consider best; 8 portions of the other
	Choice of three puddings	8 portions of one; 6 of the other two
	Cheese	Treat as an extra
Drinks parties		10 – 14 items per person
Finger buffets		8 savoury and 2 sweet items per person

Cooking plan The need to allocate adequate time to cooking for larger quantities is the key to success. I strongly recommend that you write out a detailed list of every single thing you have to prepare. Break any big jobs down into sections and include every sauce, decoration and even the bread and butter. Then estimate how long each section will take and roughly when you will get it all done. As you complete a job, cross it off the list and at the end use the lists to double-check that 'all is prepared'.

ENTERTAINING IN THE
Spring

pringtime always sneaks up on me. The weather
has been cold and damp and you have
subconsciously come to the conclusion that this year winter
will last forever. Then suddenly it is a bright sunny day,
daffodils are out, tiny buds are on every twig, a bird is
learning to fly and there is a whole new motivation
to entertain.

Just like the season, your cooking should be joyous and full
of new life and bright colours – fresh asparagus, baby sole,
spring lamb (when it becomes affordable), leeks, rhubarb
and young green herbs from the garden. How about a
drinks party to remind all your dreary friends that you still
exist and they should be entertaining you? Or a cold buffet
for Easter Day when the whole family threatens to
descend? Throw an impromptu spring lunch party or face
the day the vicar must at last come to dinner.

Spring into Action

It's not so much that you had forgotten you had invited them, more that you had not realized it was now Thursday and half past four in the afternoon to boot. Remember a dentist's appointment at work, make a quick dash to the shops and spring into action.

Just a few hours later you are totally relaxed, serving a sophisticated seasonal feast.

ICED GREEN HERB SOUP

CORONETS OF SOLE WITH ASPARAGUS SOUFFLE
NEW POTATOES
SPRING VEGETABLES

PASSION-FRUIT AND PEAR FOOL

ICED GREEN HERB SOUP

A refreshing, fragrant soup which will add a great deal of style to your dinner party, without taking too much time in the kitchen.

🕐 10 minutes, plus 2 hours for chilling
Serves 6

1 cucumber
450ml / ¾ pint thick plain yoghurt
450ml / ¾ pint cold water
1 tbsp chopped fresh chives
1 tbsp chopped parsley
1 tbsp chopped fresh tarragon
grated rind and juice of 1 lemon
175g / 6oz soft breadcrumbs
salt and freshly ground black pepper
caster sugar
chopped fresh herbs to decorate

Peel and roughly chop the cucumber; blend to a pulp in a food processor. Remove from the processor and mix with the yoghurt, water, chopped herbs and lemon. Whisk the mixture together. Now add the breadcrumbs to this watery green 'sludge' and *voilà* the soup thickens and holds. Season with salt, pepper and sugar. Chill before serving with a few extra chopped herbs sprinkled on each portion.

CORONETS OF SOLE WITH ASPARAGUS SOUFFLE

This is the ideal recipe to impress the in-laws – it sounds, looks and tastes magnificent and is terribly easy to make. The sole fillets are curled into crown shapes, filled with a little asparagus soufflé and baked in the oven.

For the vegetables, I recommend some new Jersey mids and a mixture of mangetout and baby carrots.

🕐 30 minutes, plus 10 minutes in the oven
Serves 6

6 (150–175g / 5–6oz) lemon sole fillets,
  skinned
a little melted butter
225g / 8oz asparagus, trimmed and cooked
25g / 1oz margarine
25g / 1oz plain flour
1 egg yolk
salt and freshly ground black pepper
grated nutmeg
2 egg whites
tarragon béarnaise sauce (page 28)

Preparation
Lay the sole fillets out flat on a chopping board and split them in two along the centre line. Now place two halves lengthways, overlapping to give you a band of fish about 30cm/12 inches long and 6cm/2½ inches wide. Roll the band into a cylinder shape and set it upright like a coronet on a buttered baking sheet. Repeat with the remaining fillets. If you find your cylinders will not hold their shape, use wooden cocktail sticks to skewer the joins. Brush melted butter over each fish.

Save six asparagus spears to decorate and purée the rest. Split the saved spears in two lengthways.

Melt the margarine in a small pan, stir in the flour and cook for 1 minute. Remove from the heat and cool just enough so you can hold your hand on the side of the pan.

Stir in the egg yolk, add the asparagus purée and season well. Whisk the egg whites in a separate bowl until very stiff. Fold the egg whites into the mixture and carefully spoon it into the cylinders of sole. The whole thing can now be chilled in the refrigerator for up to 2 hours before cooking and serving.

Cooking and serving

Set the oven at 180°C/350°F/gas 4. Bake the sole, uncovered, for 10 minutes. Use a fish slice to transfer the coronets to individual plates and decorate with asparagus tips. Serve with a little tarragon béarnaise sauce on each plate and offer a dish of vegetables separately.

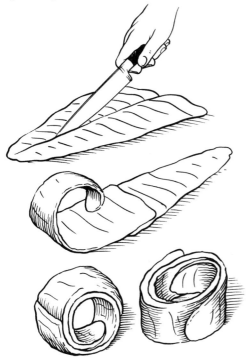

Roll each band of sole into a cylinder.

PASSION-FRUIT AND PEAR FOOL

The pear and passion-fruit complement one another beautifully in this light, tangy fool.

🕐 15 minutes, plus 2 hours for chilling
Serves 6

3 dessert pears
4 passion-fruit
2 tbsp caster sugar
300ml / ½ pint custard, home-made, carton,
  canned or instant
300ml / ½ pint double cream
fresh mint sprigs to decorate

Peel, core and purée the pears. Scoop out the seeds and flesh of the passion-fruit, saving some for decoration. Mix the two fruits with the sugar and custard. The type of custard you use depends on how lazy you are feeling. Whip the double cream to a folding consistency and fold it into the rest of the mixture. Chill well.

Serve in a large glass bowl or individual dishes. Spoon a few extra passion-fruit seeds on top and add a sprig of mint.

Home-made shortbread might be nice with it. See page 48.

25

The Easter Bunny's Buffet

Now, if the Easter bunny creeps into your garden during the night, how are we going to stop the chocolates he leaves from ruining appetites for lunch? A light, colourful buffet is required, with the chocolate egg feast scheduled immediately afterwards.

SALMON WITH SPINACH AND TARRAGON EN CROUTE
HOLLANDAISE SAUCE

....

SWEET PEPPER MOUSSE WITH QUAIL'S EGGS AND CHERRY TOMATOES
NEW POTATOES WITH YOGHURT AND MINT DRESSING
SPRING VEGETABLES VINAIGRETTE
MIXED LEAF SALAD

....

CARAMELIZED MERINGUE WITH RED AND GREEN GRAPES
RHUBARB AND ENGLISH WINE JELLY

SALMON WITH SPINACH AND TARRAGON EN CROUTE

This will make the most superb buffet centrepiece and may be served hot or cold with hollandaise sauce. I have carefully explained how to bone the salmon but, if you have got a lot of other things to prepare, it may be a case for chatting up your local fishmonger and asking him to do it for you.

🕐 1 hour, plus 25 minutes in the oven
Serves 8–10

1 (2.25kg / 5lb) salmon
450g / 1lb spinach
bunch of fresh tarragon
salt and freshly ground black pepper
grated nutmeg
450g / 1lb frozen puff pastry, thawed
egg wash (whole egg and salt mixed)
1 bunch flat-leafed parsley, 1 bunch radishes
    and 2 lemons cut into wedges to decorate
hollandaise sauce (page 28)

Boning and skinning the fish
Lay the salmon on its side and cut off its head and tail. Now insert your knife horizontally into one side of the backbone and cut all the way along the fish, feeling the bumps of the bone as you go. Then, from the inside cavity of the fish, slide your knife

under the rib cage bones and gently free the fish all the way down. One fillet should now be free – repeat this on the other side and remove the second fillet. There will be one row of bones left in each fillet which need pulling out individually.

To skin the salmon fillets, lay them skin-side down on a chopping board. Insert your knife between the flesh and skin at the tail end. Hold the end of the skin down firmly with one hand and with the other (holding your knife at a 45° angle to the board) cut all the way along evenly so that you are almost scraping the flesh off the skin.

Phew! that was an ordeal. A glass of wine now as the rest is easy.

Stuffing the fish and encasing in pastry
Blanch the spinach in boiling water for about 3 minutes. Drain thoroughly and then chop. Add the tarragon, salt, pepper and nutmeg. Lay one fillet of the salmon out flat, layer the spinach mixture evenly along it and lay the other fillet on top.

Roll out the pastry to roughly a 35 × 30-cm/ 14 × 12-inch rectangle. Lift the fish 'sandwich' on to the centre and fold the two sides of pastry over to see how it fits. We want about a 2.5-cm/1-inch overlap and spare pastry at both ends. Trim off any excess. Brush the pastry edges with water in

Cut off the head and tail, and insert the knife along the backbone.

Skin each fillet.

Lay the fish 'sandwich' on the centre of the pastry.

order to make them stick. Press the two sides firmly together and then roll the fish over on to its join.

Now for the artistry! At the tail end, gently roll the excess pastry a little wider, trim to the shape of a tail, brushing with water and seal the end with a fork. At the head end the pastry needs to be split and folded under at two angles to form a snout! Again, make sure the joins are well sealed. Mark the body of the fish with an eye, fins and scales – a large piping bag nozzle would make the perfect tool for this. Finally, brush the whole *croûte* with egg wash and lift it on to an oiled baking sheet.

Cooking and serving
Set the oven at 200°C/400°F/gas 6. Bake the fish for 25 minutes until the pastry is golden. Transfer to a suitable dish and serve cold or warm with hollandaise sauce and decorated with watercress, radishes and lemon wedges.

HOLLANDAISE SAUCE

This is an extremely useful sauce which can be served as is or used as a base for many other sauces. Here are two alternative methods for making it.

🕐 5 minutes (using a food processor); 10 minutes (by hand)
Makes about 300ml / ½ pint

6 tbsp white wine vinegar
8 egg yolks
2 tsp Dijon mustard
salt and freshly ground black pepper
225g / 8oz unsalted butter

Begin by boiling the vinegar down by two-thirds to make 2 tablespoons of liquid.

Food processor method
Put the egg yolks, mustard and plenty of salt and pepper in a food processor and blend for 1 minute. Melt the butter in a small saucepan and bring to the boil. Add the reduced vinegar to the butter and immediately pour all the liquid into the food processor with the blade running. Within a few moments the mixture should thicken. But be warned – this method will not be successful if you use fewer egg yolks or if the butter is not absolutely boiling.

Hand method
This method will take a few minutes longer than in a food processor but is more reliable and probably makes a better sauce. You can also make a half-quantity.

Put the yolks in a glass or china bowl over a saucepan of boiling water and whisk constantly, adding little knobs of butter over a period of about 5 minutes. The mixture will slowly heat and thicken. Remove the bowl from the heat and add the reduced vinegar, mustard and seasoning.

This sauce is served tepid and can either be kept in a warm place or gently reheated in a bowl over boiling water.

Other hollandaise-based sauces
Once you have mastered hollandaise, there are all sorts of other sauces you can create.

Béarnaise Add chopped chives, parsley and tarragon; for meat dishes add some of the meat juices after cooking.

Tarragon béarnaise Use tarragon vinegar instead of white wine vinegar and add chopped tarragon and cooking juices.

Maltaise Add orange juice and zest plus a tablespoon of lemon juice.

Choron Add meat juices and tomato purée.

SWEET PEPPER MOUSSE WITH QUAIL'S EGGS AND CHERRY TOMATOES

A real Easter nest, consisting of a colourful ring of savoury mousse brimming with eggs and cherry tomatoes.

🕐 30 minutes, plus 4 hours for chilling
Serves 8–10

1 red pepper
1 green pepper
1 yellow pepper
225g / 8oz cream cheese
150ml / ¼ pint mayonnaise (page 62)
grated zest and juice of ½ lemon
1 tsp Worcestershire sauce
a few drops of Tabasco
salt and freshly ground black pepper
150ml / ¼ pint medium sherry
3 tsp powdered gelatine
250ml / 8 fl oz double cream
1 round lettuce
1 punnet cherry tomatoes
12 quail's eggs, cooked and peeled
lemon slices

Oil a 1.75-litre/3-pint ring mould.

Remove the core and seeds from the peppers and dice the flesh finely. Plunge the diced pepper into a pan of boiling water for 1 minute, drain and chill immediately under the cold tap.

Mix the diced peppers, cream cheese, mayonnaise, lemon and Worcestershire sauce until completely smooth. Season well with salt, pepper and Tabasco.

Put the sherry in a small pan and sprinkle the gelatine evenly on to it. Leave to swell (that means to absorb some of the sherry) for 3 minutes, then heat gently until the gelatine has completely dissolved.

Add the sherry and gelatine mixture to the other ingredients and mix together. Whip the double cream lightly, fold this in and pour the mixture into the ring mould. Chill for 4 hours until set.

Ease the mousse gently away from the sides of the mould and then turn it out on to a serving plate. Fill the centre of the mousse with a bed of shredded lettuce and scatter the quail's eggs and cherry tomatoes on top. Arrange a complete ring of halved lemon slices around the edge.

NEW POTATOES WITH YOGHURT AND MINT DRESSING

For potato salads allow 100g / 4oz per person.

🕐 10 minutes, plus 20 minutes for cooking potatoes
Serves 8–10

900g / 2lb baby new potatoes, washed
salt for cooking
300ml / ½ pint thick plain yoghurt
1 tsp Dijon mustard
small bunch of fresh mint, finely chopped
1 tsp salt
freshly ground black pepper

Cook the potatoes in boiling salted water until tender. Drain, chill and place in a serving dish.

Mix the yoghurt with the mustard, half the mint, salt and pepper. Spoon this dressing over the potatoes and sprinkle the remaining mint on top.

SPRING VEGETABLES VINAIGRETTE

Choose the best-looking vegetables in the shop (or from your garden) to get an interesting colourful selection. These are my suggestions.

🕐 20 minutes, plus 20 minutes for cooking vegetables
Serves 8–10

450g / 1lb broccoli, cut in florets
450g / 1lb asparagus, cut in 5-cm / 2-inch
  lengths
450g / 1lb carrots, peeled and sliced in ovals
4 spring onions, sliced
1 bunch radishes, quartered
150ml / ¼ pint vinaigrette dressing (page 46)
chopped parsley

Cook the broccoli, asparagus and carrots separately so you can be sure to get them all tender but still firm. Drain and refresh under the cold tap. Place the cooked vegetables together with the spring onions and radishes in a mixing bowl. Heat the vinaigrette in a small pan and pour it over the salad while hot. Mix well, transfer to a serving dish and sprinkle with chopped parsley.

MIXED LEAF SALAD

The last of the winter's radicchio and lamb's tongue or the first round lettuces, lollo rosso or oak leaf – again, choose what looks the most attractive.

🕐 10 minutes
Serves 8–10

3 assorted lettuces
olive oil
lemon juice
salt and freshly ground black pepper

Tear the lettuces into tufts, breaking the bitter ones like radicchio and endive into smaller pieces. Sprinkle with olive oil, lemon juice, salt and pepper. Toss and arrange in a serving dish, making sure all three colours are evenly distributed.

CARAMELIZED MERINGUE WITH RED AND GREEN GRAPES

Commonsense told me this recipe would not work; pouring boiling caramel over meringue topped with whipped cream and fruit would surely be a formula for a shrivelled mess. Miraculously it *does* work and looks and tastes stunning.

🕐 25 minutes, plus 2 hours in the oven
Serves 8

Meringue
4 egg whites
225g / 8oz caster sugar
pinch of salt

Topping
300ml / ½ pint double cream
175g / 6oz seedless red grapes, washed and
  stalks removed
175g / 6oz seedless green grapes, washed
  and stalks removed

Caramel
100g / 4oz caster sugar
150ml / ¼ pint water

Set the oven at 110°C/225°F/gas ¼ and line a baking sheet with non-stick parchment paper.

I now recommend an electric mixer or a very strong arm. Whisk the whites until they are very stiff. Continue whisking while adding the caster sugar gradually, a tablespoon at a time. The whole essence of good meringue is to keep the air in and not 'flatten' it by adding sugar too quickly.

Spoon a little of the meringue mixture into a piping bag, then dollop the rest on to the baking sheet, levelling it out into a 25-cm/10-inch diameter round. Alongside the large meringue, pipe miniature meringue rosettes with the remaining mixture. Bake in the oven for 2 hours.

Transfer the large meringue to a serving plate. Whip the double cream until stiff, then spoon it on top, saving a little to sandwich together the miniature rosettes. Cover the cream with a complete layer of the two varieties of grapes and arrange the baby meringues in a cluster on the top.

Prepare the caramel by heating the sugar and water together in a heavy-based saucepan over a low heat. Do not stir the mixture at all. It will bubble away for about 12 minutes and will slowly turn from a pale colour to a deep golden brown.

As the caramel turns a nutty-brown colour, pour it quickly over the dessert. It will immediately crystallize and set – touch wood.

RHUBARB AND ENGLISH WINE JELLY

This recipe is really included as a plug for my own English vineyard and, if I am to be completely dishonest, I must warn you that the dish will never be perfect if you substitute a different wine.

🕐 30 minutes, plus 6 hours for chilling
Serves 8

675g / 1½ lb rhubarb
450ml / ¾ pint English wine
175g / 6oz caster sugar
1 cinnamon stick
grated zest and juice of 1 orange
2 tbsp elderflower cordial
25g / 1oz powdered gelatine
*whipped cream, orange segments and mint
   leaves to decorate*

Chop the rhubarb roughly and cook it in a saucepan with the wine, sugar and cinnamon stick over a gentle heat until the rhubarb is completely soft (about 20 minutes). Remove the cinnamon stick and liquidize the mixture to a purée. Add the orange and the elderflower cordial. Put about 150ml/¼ pint of the liquid in a pan and sprinkle the gelatine over. Leave for 3 minutes and then heat gently until the gelatine has completely dissolved. Stir the dissolved gelatine back into the remaining liquid and pour it into a traditional jelly mould (1-litre/2-pint capacity). Chill for at least 6 hours until set.

To turn the jelly out, I recommend you dip the mould cautiously into a basin of hot water, then place a plate on top and turn both over together.

Decorate the jelly with whipped cream, orange segments and mint leaves.

Port to the Left

I recall the first time I sat down at a formal dinner for 24 guests, all seated at one huge dining-table adorned with silver candelabra. At the close of the meal, a decanter of port was placed right in front of me. I knew I should help myself, then pass it on – but heaven only knew which way. The girl on my left seemed nice so I gave it to her. I survived – here is a dinner party to celebrate my success.

HADDOCK AND LEEK SMOKIES

ROAST LEG OF SPRING LAMB WITH APRICOT AND GINGER SAUCE
SLICED BAKED POTATOES
CARROT AND SWEDE PUREE
BROCCOLI

STILTON, WALNUT AND FIELD MUSHROOM SAVOURY

Coronet of Sole

Salmon with Spinach and Tarragon en Croûte;
Hollandaise Sauce; Sweet Pepper Mousse with
Quail's Eggs and Cherry Tomatoes;
Spring Vegetables Vinaigrette

HADDOCK AND LEEK SMOKIES

This is one of those hot starters in a ramekin which make serving very easy. This recipe tends to make 7 or 8 portions rather than 6 so there should be one available for your lunch if you want to be the guinea pig!

🕐 25 minutes, plus 10–15 minutes in the oven
Serves 6

675g / 1½lb smoked haddock fillets
600ml / 1 pint milk
225g / 8oz leeks, finely chopped
40g / 1½oz margarine
40g / 1½oz plain flour
50g / 2oz Cheddar cheese, grated
freshly ground black pepper
1 tbsp grated Parmesan cheese

Preparation
Set the oven at 200°C/400°F/gas 6.

Place the haddock in an ovenproof dish with half the milk; cover and poach in the oven for 10 minutes. Drain off the liquid and keep it to one side; remove the skin and flake the fish into a mixing bowl.

Cook the leeks in boiling water until tender (about 5 minutes). Drain and refresh under the cold tap. Mix the leeks with the flaked fish and fill the ramekins with the mixture.

Melt the margarine in a saucepan, add the flour and cook for 1 minute, stirring constantly. Remove from the heat and mix in the remaining milk, the fish cooking liquid and grated Cheddar cheese. Return the pan to the heat and bring to the boil. Season with pepper only (the fish will be salty), then pour the sauce over the haddock and leeks. Sprinkle Parmesan cheese on top.

Final cooking and serving
Set the oven at 200°C/400°F/gas 6. Place the ramekins on a baking sheet in case they bubble over and cook in the oven for 10–15 minutes until golden on top and serve.

ROAST LEG OF SPRING LAMB WITH APRICOT AND GINGER SAUCE

When the first new season's lamb comes into the shops, it is exorbitantly expensive. A couple of weeks later the excitement dies down and the price starts to drop – that's the time to put it on your menu.

🕐 20 minutes, plus 1¼ hours in the oven
Serves 6

1 (1.75kg / 4lb) leg of lamb
25g / 1oz lard
fresh rosemary sprigs

Sauce
½ onion, chopped
1 tbsp grated root ginger
1 garlic clove, crushed
40g / 1½oz plain flour
75ml / 3 fl oz white wine (English, of
  course)
50g / 2oz dried apricots, puréed
450ml / ¾ pint cold water
½ tsp garam masala
salt and freshly ground black pepper
watercress to decorate

Preparation
Put the lamb in a roasting tin with the lard and scatter the rosemary over. Gather together all the ingredients for the sauce, so you can make it when the lamb is cooked just before dinner is served.

33

Cooking and serving
Set the oven at 220°C/425°F/gas 7. Roast the lamb for 1¼ hours to serve it pink or 1½ hours to serve it fully cooked. Once cooked, drain the fat out of the roasting tin into a saucepan and keep the lamb warm. Heat the fat and cook the onion, ginger and garlic in it for 3 minutes. Stir in the flour and cook for a further minute. Stir in the white wine a little at time, then the water. Add the apricot purée, bring to the boil and season with garam masala, salt and pepper.

Transfer the meat to a carving dish and decorate it with watercress. Carve the lamb at the table and serve the sauce separately, along with some sliced baked potatoes, broccoli, and carrot and swede purée.

CARROT AND SWEDE PUREE

There are all sorts of delicious vegetable purées which can be prepared in advance and then reheated in the oven just before serving. On other occasions try celeriac or parsnip and use a little potato to help bind it together.

🕐 20 minutes, plus 20 minutes for cooking vegetables
Serves 6

450g / 1lb carrots, peeled and roughly
  chopped
450g / 1lb swede, peeled and roughly
  chopped
50g / 2oz butter
grated zest and juice of 1 small orange
2 tsp soft brown sugar
½ tsp powdered cinnamon
salt and freshly ground black pepper

Cook the carrots and swede together in a large pan of boiling salted water until they are very soft (20 minutes). Drain; then, while still hot, pass the vegetables through a mouli-grinder. Mix in the butter, orange, sugar, cinnamon and seasoning. Transfer to an ovenproof dish to re-heat when needed.

STILTON, WALNUT AND FIELD MUSHROOM SAVOURY

There is something rather grand about serving a savoury and, if we are going to pass the port, this is the perfect companion.

🕐 10 minutes, plus 8–10 minutes in the oven
Serves 6

50g / 2oz margarine
6 (10-cm / 4-inch diameter) black field
  mushrooms
175g / 6oz Stilton cheese
50g / 2oz walnuts, chopped
salt and freshly ground black pepper
6 slices of toast, buttered
chopped parsley

Preparation
Melt the margarine in a pan and lightly cook the mushrooms until softened. Transfer them on to a baking sheet gill-side up.

Crumble the Stilton and fill each mushroom with it. Sprinkle on the walnuts and season well with salt and pepper.

Cooking and serving
Set the oven at 220°C/425°F/gas 7. Bake the mushrooms for 8–10 minutes, until the cheese is bubbling. Transfer on to the hot buttered toast, sprinkle with parsley and serve immediately.

Colourful Cocktails

Not those lurid blue, orange or pink drinks served on a
Caribbean cruise ship with a forest of fruit salad
preventing you from reaching the rim of the glass, I refer to
a room full of animated, colourful people vibrating with
witty conversation, bubbles flowing and an abundance of
irresistible bite-sized eats.

HOT:
MINIATURE FILO PARCELS
BACON DEVILS WITH MUSTARD MAYONNAISE
GRUYERE CHEESE BEIGNETS

COLD:
COCKTAIL ROULADES OF WATERCRESS AND RED PEPPER
OR SMOKED SALMON AND TARRAGON
MINIATURE STUFFED VEGETABLES
PROVENCAL DIP WITH CRUDITES
MELON BASKETS OF CHARCUTERIE KEBABS

MINIATURE
FILO PARCELS

These are incredibly popular cocktail party items which can be prepared well in advance and then just popped in the oven in small batches to re-heat when needed during the party. Each variety has a different shape so you can identify the fillings.

Crab and Ginger Parcels
🕐 20 minutes
Makes 20

a little butter for cooking
2 tsp grated root ginger
1 garlic clove, crushed
100g / 4oz crab meat
2 tsp soy sauce
salt and freshly ground black pepper
175g / 6oz filo pastry
oil for frying

Melt a little butter in a small pan and fry the ginger and garlic gently. Add the crab meat and season with soy sauce, salt and pepper. Leave to cool.

Lay the filo pastry out on a work surface and cut into 10-cm/4-inch squares. Use two squares of pastry (double thickness) and place a spoonful of the crab mixture in the centre. Fold two opposite sides over the filling and then fold the remaining sides over, making a little square pillow. Moisten the join with a little water.

Heat the oil in a deep pan and fry the parcels for 2–3 minutes until golden. Transfer to an oiled baking sheet.

Duck and Mango Parcels
🕐 20 minutes
Makes 20

100g / 4oz cooked duck meat
2 tbsp mango chutney
salt and freshly ground black pepper
175g / 6oz filo pastry
oil for frying

Cut the duck into fine strips. Mix with the mango chutney and season well.

Lay the filo pastry out and cut into 13-cm/ 5-inch squares; cut these diagonally across to make triangles. Use two triangles of pastry (double thickness) and place a spoonful of the duck mixture in the centre. Brush the edges with a little water, fold the middle point of the triangle over the filling and then fold the two side points over to form a triangular parcel.

Heat the oil in a deep pan and fry the parcels for 2–3 minutes until golden. Transfer to an oiled baking sheet.

These and the crab parcels could be served with a small dish of soy sauce as a dip.

Camembert Parcels
🕐 20 minutes, plus 2 hours for chilling or freezing
Makes 20

225g / 8oz Camembert cheese
freshly ground black pepper
175g / 6oz filo pastry
oil for frying

Cut the Camembert into sticks 4 × 1 × 1cm/ 1½ × ½ × ½ inches. Season well with black pepper.

Lay the filo pastry out and cut into 13-cm/ 5-inch squares. Cut these diagonally across to make triangles. Use two triangles of pastry (double thickness) and place a stick of Camembert along the long edge. Fold the two end points in over the cheese. Moisten the remaining point of pastry and then roll the cheese up, making a long stick-shaped parcel. Chill well or freeze.

Heat the oil in a deep pan and fry the parcels for 2–3 minutes until golden. Transfer to an oiled baking sheet.

BACON DEVILS WITH MUSTARD MAYONNAISE

Moments to prepare but resulting in a tasty, crunchy canapé that all your guests will talk about – favourably, I hope.

🕐 10 minutes, plus 10 minutes in the oven
Makes about 16–20 canapés

225g / 8oz streaky bacon rashers, rinds removed
1 (425g / 15oz) can water chestnuts

Mustard Mayonnaise
150ml / ¼ pint mayonnaise (page 62)
2 tsp coarse-grain mustard
1 tsp Worcestershire sauce
1 tsp clear honey

Set the oven at 200°C/400°F/gas 6.

Stretch out the bacon rashers, cut into two and wrap a water chestnut in each length. Place on a wire rack with a baking sheet under it and cook in the oven for 10 minutes.

Mix all the other ingredients together to make the mustard mayonnaise and serve it alongside the warm bacon devils.

GRUYERE CHEESE BEIGNETS

I always describe *beignets* as just a fancy French version of doughnuts, although they are made from deep-fried choux pastry rather than dough. These small savoury doughnuts can be fried in advance and then re-heated at the party.

🕐 25 minutes, including frying
Makes about 20

150ml / ¼ pint cold water
50g / 2oz butter, cut in small pieces
50g / 2oz plain flour
2 eggs
100g / 4oz Gruyère cheese, grated
salt and freshly ground black pepper
a few drops of Tabasco
oil for frying
25g / 1oz Parmesan cheese, grated

Heat the water and butter together and bring to the boil. As this mixture bubbles up the pan, remove it from the heat and immediately add all the flour. Stir vigorously until the mixture becomes a smooth lump. Allow this to cool slightly, then beat in the eggs a little at a time. Continue to beat for 2–3 minutes, add the Gruyère cheese and season well with salt, pepper and Tabasco. Pipe the mixture on to an oiled baking sheet to form even rounds.

Heat a pan of deep oil to a medium (not high) temperature. Using a palette knife, drop the choux rounds into the oil to cook. Cook a few at a time for 6 minutes per batch. Scoop the cooked beignets out of the oil and roll them in the Parmesan cheese to dry and coat.

COCKTAIL ROULADES OF WATERCRESS AND RED PEPPER OR SMOKED SALMON AND TARRAGON

Miniature savoury roulades make an ideal cocktail party dish. They look delightful and each roulade makes 20 little canapés – that must be a plus.

I have included recipes for both a watercress and a smoked salmon roulade but many other varieties are also possible.

Watercress and Red Pepper Roulade

🕐 30 minutes, plus 8 minutes in the oven and 2 hours for chilling
Makes 20 canapés

1½ bunches watercress
3 eggs, separated
salt and freshly ground black pepper
a few drops of lemon juice
1 tbsp grated Parmesan cheese
100g / 4oz cream cheese
a little milk
1 red pepper, finely diced

Set the oven at 200°C/400°F/gas 6. Oil a Swiss roll tin and line it with baking parchment.

Chop the watercress finely either by hand or in a food processor. Mix it with the egg yolks and season well with salt, pepper and lemon juice. Whisk the egg whites in a separate bowl until stiff. Fold the whites into the watercress mixture, using a metal spoon. Spoon the mixture into the prepared tin and take care to spread it very evenly right to the edges. Sprinkle on the Parmesan cheese and bake for 8 minutes. Leave the roulade to cool.

Turn the roulade out on to a sheet of greaseproof paper and peel the baking parchment off the back. Blend the cream

cheese with a little milk to obtain a smooth spreading consistency. Spread this on to the roulade and then sprinkle evenly with the diced red pepper. Now, using the greaseproof paper to help you, make a first tight tuck in the roulade. After that it should be (?) easy – roll the roulade up firmly to resemble a Swiss roll. Chill in the refrigerator before slicing into 20 beautiful little green, white and red rondelles.

Use a sheet of greaseproof paper to roll up the roulade.

Slice into rondelles.

Smoked Salmon and Tarragon Roulade

🕐 30 minutes, plus 8 minutes in the oven and 2 hours for chilling
Makes 20 canapés

100g / 4oz smoked salmon pieces
3 eggs, separated
salt and freshly ground black pepper
a few drops of tarragon vinegar
1 tbsp grated Parmesan cheese
100g / 4oz cream cheese
a little milk
chopped fresh tarragon

Follow the method exactly as for the watercress and red pepper roulade (above) but substitute the smoked salmon for the watercress and the tarragon vinegar for the lemon juice. Sprinkle with chopped tarragon.

It's well worth the bother of making both types of roulade and arranging them alternately on your serving dish.

MINIATURE STUFFED VEGETABLES

I know what you are going to say: 'much too fiddly for me' but, if I can only persuade you to have a go, you will be so pleased with yourself that you will parade these canapés around your cocktail party like a peacock showing off his plumes.

Cherry Tomatoes
🕐 5 minutes to 2 hours, depending on your expertise
Makes about 20 canapés

1 punnet cherry tomatoes
75g / 3oz cream cheese
1 tsp pesto sauce
a little fresh basil

Using a very sharp knife, cut a little skin off the stalk end of the tomato so it will sit flat. Now cut the top quarter off the other end. Scoop out the tomato seeds. Mix the cream cheese with the pesto sauce and then pipe the mixture into each tomato. Place a tiny leaf or sliver of basil on top of the filling and replace the top like a little hat at a 'rakish' angle.

Mangetout
🕐 5 minutes to 2 hours, depending on your expertise
Makes about 20 canapés

20 mangetout
75g / 3oz cream cheese
a few fresh chives, finely snipped

Blanch the mangetout in boiling water for 30 seconds, then drain and refresh under the cold tap. Using a fine pointed knife, cut a small piece off the end, then insert the knife into the pod and split it open along one side.

Using a fine nozzle, pipe the cream cheese into each mangetout with a gentle up-and-down motion like drawing a wiggly worm. Sprinkle a few chopped chives on top.

Button Mushrooms
🕐 5 minutes to 2 hours, depending on your expertise
Makes about 20 canapés

20 small button mushrooms
75g / 3oz cream cheese
fresh parsley, both chopped and sprigs
freshly ground black pepper
grated nutmeg

Remove the stalks from the mushrooms and slice a little off the domes carefully so they will sit flat. Mix the cream cheese with chopped parsley, pepper and nutmeg. Pipe this into the cups of the mushrooms and decorate each with a little parsley sprig.

Other Stuffed Vegetables
There are all sorts of other vegetables you can trim and stuff in similar ways. Try cucumber boats, young celery, artichoke hearts, scooped-out radishes and so on.

PROVENCAL DIP WITH CRUDITES

A spicy mushroom dip which may be handed round or left on the side for guests to help themselves.

🕐 30 minutes
Makes about 600ml / 1 pint – suitable for 20 people

25g / 1oz margarine
450g / 1lb black flat mushrooms, puréed
2 garlic cloves, crushed
2 tsp Worcestershire sauce
salt and freshly ground black pepper
a few drops of Tabasco
200ml / 7 fl oz mayonnaise (page 62)
2 tbsp tomato purée

Crudités
1 head celery
450g / 1lb carrots, peeled
1 cucumber
1 red pepper
1 yellow pepper

Melt the margarine in a frying pan and cook the puréed mushrooms and garlic together for 5 minutes. Stir in the Worcestershire sauce and season well with salt, pepper and a few drops of Tabasco (careful!). Leave to cool. Once cold, blend the mushroom mixture with the mayonnaise and tomato purée and transfer to a serving dish.

The crudités can comprise any raw vegetables you like; my suggestions above are just examples. Cut the vegetables into even strips about 7.5cm/3 inches long.

Place the dip in the centre of a large platter or tray and arrange the different vegetables in bundles around it.

MELON BASKETS OF CHARCUTERIE KEBABS

This is a very simple but effective idea: little cocktail sticks holding different salamis and cured meats (all bought from a delicatessen) served in and around a melon basket.

🕐 30 minutes
Makes about 40 canapés

1 large honeydew melon
10 thin slices garlic sausage
10 thin slices Bresaola
5 thin slices salami
5 thin slices Parma ham
cocktail onions and gherkins (optional)

Cut a little skin off each end of the melon and mark a line all the way round the middle. Now 'star cut' (that sounds professional) the melon into two halves by stabbing a sharp knife into it in a zigzag pattern all the way around the guideline.

Scoop the seeds out of each side of the melon, then carefully cut out the flesh, leaving the two skins as 'baskets'. Cut the melon flesh into small chunks and place a piece of melon and a folded slice of charcuterie on each cocktail stick. The larger slices of charcuterie should be cut in half.

To add variety to these canapés, you can make some kebabs substituting a miniature cocktail onion or gherkin for melon.

Place the melon baskets filled with prepared kebabs on a serving plate and arrange the other kebabs in clusters around.

Roast Leg of Spring Lamb with Apricot
and Ginger Sauce

Selection of hot and cold canapés

Simply Asparagus

Elderflower Custard with Fresh Fruit

Vegetarians Aren't All Bad

Of course that is a matter of opinion and, as a professional chef faced with an expanding requirement for non-meat, non-fish and non-milk dishes, I am not always sure! Especially when in sight of a delicious slice of roast beef, the dietary principles suddenly fall by the wayside – 'just for today'.

Vegetarian food, however, can be as exciting and varied as any meat or fish dish and a vegetarian dinner party may be just what is needed.

MEDITERRANEAN ARTICHOKE HEARTS

SPICY HAZELNUT KOULIBIACA
SPRING VEGETABLES

BAKED LEMON PUDDING
WITH BRANDY ORANGE COULIS

MEDITERRANEAN ARTICHOKE HEARTS

A truly Mediterranean flavour makes this an inspired starter. Sun-dried tomatoes are imported from Italy, sold in jars and marinated in olive oil .

🕐 20 minutes, plus 8–10 minutes in the oven
Serves 6

2–3 (425g / 15oz) cans artichoke hearts, drained
3 sun-dried tomatoes, finely chopped
100g / 4oz goat's cheese
75g / 3oz cream cheese
2 tsp pesto sauce
a little milk
freshly ground black pepper
100g / 4oz lamb's tongue salad, washed and torn into tufts
1 oak leaf lettuce, washed and torn into tufts
12 cherry tomatoes, quartered
a few basil leaves, if available
olive oil
lemon juice
salt and freshly ground black pepper

Preparation

Begin by cutting a little off the base of each artichoke in order to sit them upright. Using your thumbs, mould the tops into little cups. Set them ready on a baking sheet.

Mix the sun-dried tomatoes, goat's cheese, cream cheese and pesto together and moisten the mixture with a little milk. Season with pepper. Fill each artichoke heart with this mixture.

Dress the two different lettuce leaves lightly with oil, lemon juice, salt and pepper and arrange them as nests on individual starter plates. Dot the cherry tomato quarters and basil leaves around on top.

Cooking and serving

Set the oven at 220°C/425°F/gas 7.

Bake the artichokes for 8–10 minutes; arrange three in each salad nest and serve. I can smell them now – delicious!

SPICY HAZELNUT KOULIBIACA

Koulibiaca is an eastern European dish which usually comprises rice, egg and fish encased in pastry. In this recipe we are replacing the fish with hazelnuts and sweet peppers. I would accompany this with some crisp spring vegetables.

🕐 40 minutes, plus 25 minutes in the oven
Serves 6

25g / 1oz margarine
1 medium onion, chopped
2 red peppers, seeded and diced
175g / 6oz hazelnuts, roughly chopped
175g / 6oz rice, cooked
3 hard-boiled eggs, chopped
2 tbsp chopped parsley
1 tsp chilli sauce
2 tsp tomato purée
2 tsp Worcestershire sauce
salt and freshly ground black pepper
350g / 12oz frozen puff pastry, thawed
egg wash (whole egg and salt mixed)
watercress sprigs to decorate
300ml / ½ pint thick soured cream, seasoned with salt and pepper, to serve

Preparation

Melt the margarine in a pan and cook the onion and peppers until soft. Add the hazelnuts and cook for another minute or so, then remove from the heat. Now add the rice, egg and parsley and season with chilli sauce, tomato purée, Worcestershire sauce, salt and pepper. Mix all the ingredients together and leave to cool.

Roll out the puff pastry to a rectangle about 35 × 23cm/14 × 9 inches. Spoon the mixture down the centre and then fold over the two sides to make a cylinder. Brush the pastry where it overlaps and at each end with water. Seal the ends by pressing the pastry together with a fork. Roll the whole thing over so the seal is underneath. Brush with egg wash and transfer to a baking sheet. Chill until needed.

Cooking and serving
Set the oven at 200°C/400°F/gas 6.

Bake the koulibiaca for 25 minutes just before dinner, then keep it warm for about 15 minutes before serving. Decorate with sprigs of watercress and cut into portions at the table. Serve with seasoned soured cream.

BAKED LEMON PUDDING WITH BRANDY ORANGE COULIS

This traditional-style, baked pudding is very easy to make in a food processor. You can make it by hand with a little more time and effort spent whisking.

🕐 20 minutes, plus 1½ hours in the oven
Serves 6

100g / 4oz butter
225g / 8oz caster sugar
grated rind and juice of 2 lemons
4 eggs, separated
100g / 4oz self-raising flour
150ml / ¼ pint milk
icing sugar to dust
brandy orange coulis (see below)

Preparation
Put the butter, sugar and lemon rind in a food processor and blend together. Continue to process while slowly adding first the yolks, then the flour, the lemon juice and, finally, the milk. Continue to process until there is no sign of curdling, then transfer the mixture to a bowl.

Whisk the egg whites in a separate bowl until stiff. Fold these into the mixture and pour it into a buttered soufflé dish. The pudding may be kept in the refrigerator for up to 2 hours until you are ready to cook.

Cooking and Serving
Set the oven at 160°C/325°F/gas 3.

Place the soufflé dish in a roasting tin half-filled with cold water. Bake for 1½ hours, then dust with icing sugar and serve hot with brandy orange coulis.

Brandy Orange Coulis
To be lazy, I buy freshly squeezed orange juice and just grate the zest off an extra orange.

🕐 10 minutes
Makes about 450ml / ¾ pint

300ml / ½ pint freshly squeezed orange juice
grated zest of 1 orange
1 tbsp lemon juice
1 tbsp caster sugar
2 tbsp arrowroot mixed in 150ml / ¼ pint
  cold water
brandy to taste

Put the orange juice and zest, lemon juice and caster sugar in a pan and bring to the boil. Stir in the arrowroot and water mixture. Cook for a few moments until the sauce thickens, then remove from the heat and add brandy to taste. This sauce may be served warm or cold.

Lunch with Friends

To my mind, of all the occasions we entertain, an informal lunch should be the most effortless. A single main dish (not too heavy), salads, fruits, cheese and a light flavoursome wine are all that is required.

SIMPLY ASPARAGUS

OR

SALADE NICOISE

OR

FETTUCINI WITH BACON AND SAGE

OR

CARAMELIZED LEEK AND ONION TART

ELDERFLOWER CUSTARD WITH FRESH FRUIT
AND SHORTBREAD

SIMPLY ASPARAGUS

Near my home in West Sussex there are ten acres of asparagus which, from the end of April to mid-June, create a truly gastronomic landscape. No foliage or other sign of life precedes the sticks growing; they simply pop up out of the rich brown soil overnight, waiting to be dangled, dripping with melted butter, in front of greedy mouths. This dish is a celebration of asparagus; three different preparations on one plate.

🕐 45 minutes
Serves 6

Asparagus Bundles:
450g / 1lb 'select' asparagus
1 red pepper
vinaigrette dressing (page 46)

Asparagus Mousses:
100g / 4oz asparagus
100g / 4oz cream cheese
1½ tsp powdered gelatine
4 tbsp English white wine
salt and freshly ground black pepper
a few drops of Worcestershire sauce
a few drops of lemon juice
150ml / ¼ pint double cream

Asparagus Eggs:
3 hard-boiled eggs
3 asparagus spears
2 tsp mayonnaise (page 62)
1 tsp Dijon mustard

To decorate:
flat-leafed parsley

Begin by cooking all the asparagus together in boiling water for 6–8 minutes until it is tender but still firm. Drain and immediately refresh the spears in iced water; drain them again.

Asparagus Bundles
Now put to one side the asparagus needed for the mousses and eggs. Dress the remainder with a little vinaigrette. Arrange the spears in six equal bundles on a serving dish. Cut a side off the red pepper and, placing the piece flat on your chopping board, trim off some of the inside flesh. Now cut even strips of the pepper skin about 5mm/¼ inch wide and 10cm/4 inches long. Curl the strips in your fingers like rolling up a ribbon and then 'clip' them around the asparagus bundles as 'ties'.

Asparagus Mousses
To prepare the mixture, first purée the asparagus (you may need to moisten it with half the white wine). Blend the purée well with the cream cheese. Season with salt and pepper, Worcestershire sauce and lemon juice.

Put the rest of the white wine in a small saucepan and sprinkle the gelatine over. Leave to swell for 3 minutes, then heat gently until all the gelatine has dissolved.

Add the dissolved gelatine to the asparagus mixture and combine thoroughly. In a separate bowl, whip the double cream lightly and fold this into the asparagus mixture. Pour into six oiled ramekin dishes and chill in the refrigerator until set – allow 2–3 hours.

To turn out the mousses, ease them away gently from the sides of the ramekins, hold them upside-down on the palm of your hand and 'flick' – it's all in the wrist! If the moulds were very well oiled they should come out successfully.

Place a mousse between each bundle of asparagus on the platter and cut little diamonds of red pepper to decorate – two on each mousse.

Asparagus Eggs

Finally, the eggs – halve the hard-boiled eggs and scoop out the yolks. Save the tips of the asparagus; roughly chop the rest and add it to the yolks. Mix in the mayonnaise and mustard, then carefully spoon this mixture back into the egg whites. Split each tip in two lengthways and arrange these on top.

Place the eggs in a cluster in the centre of your dish and decorate with a couple of sprigs of flat-leafed parsley.

There you have it – simply asparagus.

SALADE NICOISE

A Niçoise salad gives me the perfect excuse to include a recipe for a good vinaigrette dressing. It is also one of my favourite lunch dishes – a complete meal on one plate that only needs some crunchy white bread and butter as an accompaniment.

🕐 30 minutes
Serves 6

225g / 8oz French beans
6 medium tomatoes
1 cucumber
20 black olives, pitted and halved
1 (425g / 15oz) can tuna fish, drained
4 hard-boiled eggs
1 (100g / 4oz) can anchovy fillets
chopped parsley
vinaigrette dressing (see below)

Top, tail and halve the French beans. Cook them in boiling salted water until quite soft. (For some reason I prefer a soft bean in a Niçoise to a crunchy one – you may decide otherwise.) Drain and refresh the beans under the cold tap.

Quarter the tomatoes and scoop out the pips. Cut each tomato quarter into strips of a similar size to the French beans. Peel the cucumber and again cut it into 'julienne' strips, the same length as the other vegetables – all these fancy words I am teaching you: 'julienne' strips refer to the preparation of almost anything cut to the shape of an upmarket slim chip!

Mix the beans, tomato and cucumber together with the black olives and tuna fish and dress generously with vinaigrette dressing (below). Arrange the salad on a serving dish and decorate with quartered hard-boiled eggs, little crosses of anchovy and chopped parsley.

Vinaigrette Dressing

It is well worth taking trouble over making a good vinaigrette. You can then keep a bottle in the refrigerator.

🕐 10 minutes
Makes about 300ml / ½ pint

150ml / ¼ pint olive oil
150ml / ¼ pint sunflower or groundnut oil
1 shallot, finely chopped
1 garlic clove, crushed
3 tbsp white wine vinegar
1 tbsp lemon juice
1 tbsp Dijon mustard
chopped fresh thyme
chopped fresh marjoram
salt and freshly ground black pepper
caster sugar

Heat the two oils in a pan and fry the shallot and garlic lightly for not more than 1 minute. Remove from the heat and stir in the vinegar, lemon juice and mustard. Add the chopped herbs and season well with salt, pepper and caster sugar. Allow time for the flavours to develop before using.

FETTUCINI WITH BACON AND SAGE

Don't get me wrong – I love Spag Bol and I would happily eat it two or three times a week. There are, however, occasions when a slightly more sophisticated pasta dish is called for.

🕐 30 minutes
Serves 6

25g / 1oz margarine
350g / 12oz bacon rashers, rinds removed
* and chopped*
1 medium onion, finely chopped
1 garlic clove, crushed
40g / 1½oz plain flour
600ml / 1 pint chicken stock
150ml / ¼ pint Marsala (sherry would do)
150ml / ¼ pint single cream
2 tbsp white wine vinegar
2 tbsp chopped fresh sage
salt and freshly ground black pepper
450g / 1lb fettucini
freshly grated Parmesan cheese
chopped parsley

Melt the margarine in a pan and cook the bacon, onion and garlic for 5 minutes. Stir in the flour and cook for a further minute. Stir in the stock, Marsala, cream and vinegar. Add the sage and season well. Remove from the heat and re-heat without boiling when needed.

When cooking the pasta, I recommend you add a couple of spoonfuls of olive oil to the cooking water and then two more spoonfuls of oil to the pasta as soon as it is drained.

Toss the cooked pasta in the hot bacon sauce and serve with a mixture of fresh Parmesan and chopped parsley to sprinkle on top.

CARAMELIZED LEEK AND ONION TART

This 'moreish' savoury-but-sweet tart will be a great hit for lunch, supper or just in between.

🕐 40 minutes, plus 35 minutes in the oven
Serves 6

450g / 1lb shortcrust pastry
225g / 8oz prepared onion, sliced
2 tbsp oil
225g / 8oz prepared leeks, sliced
salt and freshly ground black pepper
grated nutmeg
1 tbsp demerara sugar
2 tbsp plain flour
150ml / ¼ pint milk
150ml / ¼ pint single cream
3 eggs
2 tbsp demerara sugar for the topping

Set the oven at 200°C/400°F/gas 6.

Roll out the pastry and fit it into a 25-cm/ 10-inch oiled flan tin. Bake the case blind (page 80) before filling.

Fry the sliced onions in the oil until soft; add the leeks and continue cooking for a further 5 minutes. Season with salt, pepper and nutmeg. Add 1 tablespoon of demerara sugar, then stir in the flour to bind the mixture. Spoon the whole lot into your cooked pastry case.

Mix the milk, cream and eggs together. Pour this custard over the onion mixture until the tart is very full. Bake for 35 minutes.

Remove the tart from the oven and immediately sprinkle over the extra demerara and place under a hot grill for less than a minute to give a crunchy 'brûlée' topping. At this stage you will not be able to resist trying a slice, so make two – one for the lunch party and one for sampling.

ELDERFLOWER CUSTARD WITH FRESH FRUIT

I am never sure whether you need go to the trouble of producing a pudding for an informal lunch. Some fresh fruit and nice cheeses would be quite satisfactory but this unusual little dish is a good compromise. A delicious custard which your guests can simply dip into or spoon over fresh fruit as they wish.

🕐 25 minutes
Serves 6

3 nectarines, 175g / 6oz strawberries,
1 Galia melon or other fresh fruit of your
choice

Custard
150ml / ¼ pint milk
150ml / ¼ pint double cream
2 tbsp caster sugar
2 egg yolks
2 tbsp elderflower cordial
1 tbsp cornflour mixed in a little cold water

Prepare the fruit and cut into slices.

Heat the milk and cream together and bring to the boil. Blend the sugar and yolks in a mixing bowl, then pour the boiling milk and cream over them, stirring vigorously. Return the mixture to the pan over a gentle heat. Add the elderflower cordial and then the cornflour. Continue to stir until the custard thickens but, on no account, let it boil.

Transfer the cooked custard to a serving bowl or tiny individual bowls and serve with the prepared slices of fresh fruit.

❦

SHORTBREAD

Of course you can get shortbread out of a packet but think how virtuous you'll feel if you make it yourself!

🕐 10 minutes, plus 20 minutes in the oven
Makes 12–16 biscuits

175g / 6oz unsalted butter
100g / 4oz caster sugar
250g / 9oz plain flour
grated zest of 1 orange
extra caster sugar for sprinkling

Set the oven at 180°C/350°F/gas 4. Oil and line a Swiss roll tin with baking parchment.

Beat the butter and sugar in a bowl until quite smooth. Add the flour and grated orange zest. Spoon the mixture into the lined tin and press it out evenly. Bake for 20 minutes.

Once out of the oven and while still warm, cut the shortbread in the tin into fingers or triangles and sprinkle with caster sugar. Leave to cool completely before removing from the tin.

❦

Watermelon Boats with Italian Seafood Salad;
Escalope of Chicken with Raspberries

Tapas; Seafood Paella

ENTERTAINING IN THE
Summer

*A*n English summer is the most perfect time for parties. There are picnics and barbecues, Wimbledon and Ascot, school holidays and friends from abroad. Inevitably, on the day you choose to entertain, it always rains – you end up clustered round a table indoors but having every bit as good a time.

Any sensible book about summer parties would carefully warn you to have a wet and dry weather plan. My attitude is, of course, quite the opposite. Go the whole hog for a glorious sunny day or balmy night. If it doesn't work out, you are bound to think of something and, if it does, you will not have wasted time on all the pessimistic planning!

Food in the summer should be light, easy to eat and take full advantage of all the fresh produce available. Bountiful salads, lots of fresh fish, white meat and the wonderful soft fruits and berries. I have suggested some different ideas for the barbecue, a Mediterranean night to remind you of your holiday and all sorts of summer suppers with friends.

Your Fairy Godmother

Haven't you ever wished that your fairy godmother would just come along in the night and in the morning you would find everything perfectly prepared? Leave all the ingredients somewhere accessible together with a pumpkin if you fancy a golden coach as well.

Just in case this does not work I have devised a menu which is so easy and yet so visual and delectable your guests will refuse to believe you haven't got a fairy godmother.

WATERMELON BOATS WITH ITALIAN SEAFOOD SALAD

....

ESCALOPE OF CHICKEN WITH RASPBERRIES
JERSEY NEW POTATOES
CRISP GREEN SALAD

....

MOCHA AND PRALINE ICE-CREAM
WITH RICH CHOCOLATE SAUCE

WATERMELON BOATS WITH ITALIAN SEAFOOD SALAD

What a start to summer – the refreshing sensation of watermelon (I can hardly call it taste) combined with an Italian-style seafood salad.

🕐 30 minutes
Serves 6

1 small watermelon
½ cucumber, cut into chunks
chopped parsley and watercress sprigs to
  decorate

Seafood Salad
175ml / 6 fl oz olive oil
3 garlic cloves, crushed
450g / 1lb baby squid, cleaned and cut into
  small discs
450g / 1lb peeled prawns, drained
1 (225g / 8oz) can tuna or crab, drained
1 green chilli, very finely chopped
salt and freshly ground black pepper
2 tsp caster sugar
1 tbsp chopped fresh oregano
2 tbsp wine vinegar

Heat the olive oil in a pan and cook the garlic and the squid for 3–4 minutes. Add the prawns, tuna or crab and chilli, then season well with salt, pepper, sugar and chopped oregano. Cook for just a minute. Remove from the heat and stir in the wine vinegar. Leave to cool.

Cut the watermelon into eight long 'boats' and then cut the flesh away from the skin. Arrange the eight skins on a round serving dish in a pattern to resemble a star. Dice the watermelon flesh, removing some of the seeds (you will have too much watermelon for the salad, so it requires a combination of discarding some of the very seedy sections

and guzzling all the time you are preparing this dish).

Mix the remaining melon flesh with the cucumber and cooled seafood mixture. Spoon this into and over the melon-skin boats and pour on all the juices. Sprinkle with chopped parsley and decorate with watercress.

ESCALOPE OF CHICKEN WITH RASPBERRIES

This tangy, summery main course takes only a few minutes to produce and needs nothing but some new potatoes and a crisp green salad to go with it.

🕐 30 minutes
Serves 6

4 (225g / 8oz) chicken breasts
a little oil for frying
1 garlic clove, crushed
150ml / ¼ pint white wine
300ml / ½ pint chicken stock
1 tbsp raspberry vinegar
1 tbsp lemon juice
2 tsp caster sugar
salt and freshly ground black pepper
1 tbsp arrowroot
100g / 4oz raspberries
fresh chervil to decorate

Cut each of the chicken breasts into three thin slices. Place these under a sheet of greaseproof paper and lightly hammer them flat with a rolling pin or meat hammer. Heat a very little oil in a frying pan and fry the chicken pieces on both sides. Add the garlic while frying. Make the sure the chicken is cooked through, then transfer it to a serving dish and keep warm. Pour the white wine, chicken stock, vinegar, lemon juice and sugar into the same pan and bring to the boil. Taste and season well.

Mix the arrowroot with a little cold water and stir this into the hot liquid to thicken it. Finally, stir in the raspberries. Pour the sauce over the chicken escalopes, decorate with chervil and serve with some boiled Jersey potatoes and a crisp green salad.

MOCHA AND PRALINE ICE-CREAM WITH RICH CHOCOLATE SAUCE

A rich home-made ice-cream that requires no ice-cream makers and no repeated whisking in the freezer – you simply make it, freeze it and then eat it with a rich chocolate sauce.

🕐 40 minutes, plus 6 hours for freezing
Serves 6

Praline
100g / 4oz sweet whole almonds
100g / 4oz caster sugar

Ice-Cream
6 egg yolks
225g / 8oz caster sugar
4 tbsp instant coffee granules
150ml / ¼ pint milk
300ml / ½ pint double cream

Rich Chocolate Sauce *(see below)*

Praline
Put the almonds and sugar in a heavy-based pan over a low heat. Stir occasionally and allow the sugar to melt, then bubble to a deep nutty-brown colour. Pour the mixture

on to an oiled baking sheet and leave to cool and set hard. Break into lumps and chop in a food processor or liquidizer.

Ice-cream
Using an electric mixer, beat the yolks and sugar together until they double in volume and turn pale in colour. Put the milk and instant coffee granules into a pan and bring to the boil; then pour into the egg yolk and sugar mixture and beat for another 3 minutes. Whip the cream in a separate bowl until stiff and then fold it into the rest of the mixture. Stir in half the praline and transfer to a serving dish and freeze for at least 6 hours.

Remove the ice-cream from the freezer a good 10 minutes before you want to serve it. Sprinkle the remaining praline in a layer over the top.

Rich Chocolate Sauce
The principle of a good chocolate sauce is very simple – you have to mix the chocolate with water to enable it to melt without coagulating. Then you boil away the water to thicken the chocolate again.

🕐 20 minutes
Makes about 300ml / ½ pint

225g / 8oz bitter chocolate
300ml / ½ pint cold water
100g / 4oz caster sugar

Break the chocolate into small pieces and put it, together with the water and sugar, in a heavy-based pan. Place over a moderate heat and bring to the boil, stirring occasionally. Continue to boil (without boiling over – easily done, I warn you) until the sauce sticks to a spoon. Transfer to another container; allow to cool or serve warm.

Costa del Basildon

Out with the souvenir sombreros, jugs of sangria and an old copy of *Y Viva España* but, instead of the hamburgers and egg and chips normally offered on the Costas, let's produce some really lovely traditional Spanish fare.

Authentic Spanish cuisine is as varied and colourful as that of Italy or France; the difference is they try to keep it for themselves.

TAPAS

....

SEAFOOD PAELLA

....

FRESH FRUITS WITH MANCHEGO

TAPAS

To serve tapas properly, they must be laid out on a long 'bar' and offered with pre-dinner drinks for guests to help themselves. The drinking and snacking goes on for a long time before 'moving on' and sitting down for dinner. The food itself should be as varied and colourful as possible, ranging from little dishes of olives and garlic new potatoes to scallops and fried fish. I have suggested a range of dishes to make a good display.

🕐 Allow 1 hour and see how many you have made
Serves 8–10

Spanish Olives
50g / 2oz black olives
50g / 2oz green olives
1 tbsp olive oil
1 garlic clove, crushed
1 tbsp chopped fresh oregano
salt and freshly ground black pepper

Roll the olives in the oil, garlic, oregano and seasoning.

Marinated Sun-dried Tomatoes and Mushrooms
50g / 2oz sun-dried tomatoes, cut into strips
100g / 4oz mushrooms, thinly sliced
1 garlic clove, crushed
1 tbsp sherry vinegar
2 tbsp olive oil, taken from the tomato jar
salt and freshly ground black pepper

Mix all the ingredients together and leave for 2 hours before serving.

Roasted Peppers
1 red pepper
1 green pepper
1 yellow pepper
2 tbsp olive oil
salt and freshly ground black pepper

Set the oven at 240°C/475°F/gas 9.

Cut the sides off the peppers, discarding the inner pith and core, and lay them skin-side up on an oiled baking tin. Brush with olive oil and bake for 5 minutes until the skin burns and blisters. Scrape off the skin and cut the flesh into long strips. Mix together and season with salt and pepper.

Chorizo Sausage or Serano Ham
Simply sliced and served on a small dish.

Scallops with Onions
2 tbsp olive oil
1 white onion, chopped
1 garlic clove, crushed
225g / 8oz scallops
salt and freshly ground black pepper
chopped parsley

Heat the oil in a pan and cook the onion and garlic until soft. Add the scallops, season well and cook for 2–3 minutes until the fish is opaque. Transfer to a small serving dish and sprinkle with parsley.

Baby New Potatoes
450g / 1lb small new potatoes
2 garlic cloves, crushed
olive oil
wine vinegar
salt and freshly ground black pepper

Boil the potatoes in salted water until tender. Drain and, while still hot, add the garlic and dress to taste with olive oil, wine vinegar and salt and pepper. Allow to cool.

Fried Fish
100g / 4oz cod, cut into slices
6–12 king prawns, peeled
50g / 2oz plain flour
salt and freshly ground black pepper
oil for frying
1 lemon, cut into wedges

Coat the cod and prawns in seasoned flour, then fry in hot oil for 2–3 minutes. Serve with lemon wedges and don't worry if the fish gets cold.

Kidneys in Balsamic Vinegar
2 tbsp olive oil
225g / 8oz calves or lambs kidney, trimmed and sliced
2 garlic cloves, crushed
1 tbsp balsamic vinegar
4 tbsp white wine
1 tbsp tomato purée
salt and freshly ground black pepper
cayenne pepper
chopped parsley

Heat the oil in a pan until it is very hot, then fry the kidneys and garlic for 3–4 minutes. Remove the kidneys and transfer to a serving dish. Add the vinegar, wine and tomato purée to the pan, season well, then pour the mixture over the kidneys. Sprinkle cayenne pepper and chopped parsley on top.

SEAFOOD PAELLA

This is one of those glorious foods which provides a talking point, a table centrepiece and the whole meal in one dish. There are no shortcuts; it starts with making a proper chicken stock and ends with adding as much variety of fish, seafood, ham, sausage and vegetables as you can come up with. The only essential is a paella pan (an extra-wide frying pan).

🕐 3 hours to cook chicken and stock,
1 hour to prepare and cook paella
Serves 8–10

1 (1.75kg / 4lb) chicken
vegetables, such as onion, carrot and celery, roughly chopped
bay-leaf, thyme, peppercorns and garlic cloves

Paella
75ml / 3 fl oz olive oil
1 large white onion, chopped
2 garlic cloves, crushed
1 red pepper, diced
1 green pepper, diced
350g / 12oz long-grain rice
1½ tsp ground turmeric
salt and freshly ground black pepper
2 chorizo sausages, sliced
1 (400g / 14oz) can artichoke hearts, drained
1 (400g / 14oz) can tomatoes
450g / 1lb mussels in their shells
225g / 8oz squid, prepared and cut into rings
12 king prawns
2 lemons
chopped parsley

Chicken stock
Place the chicken in a large saucepan with some suitable vegetables, a bay-leaf, sprigs

of thyme, peppercorns and garlic. Cover completely with water (about 1.75 litres/ 3 pints). Bring to the boil, simmer for 45 minutes and then remove the bird from the pot. Allow the chicken to cool slightly before removing all the flesh from the bones. Cut the flesh into strips and chill until needed. Return the bones to the stock and continue to simmer for a further 2 hours.

At the end of the cooking time, pour the stock through a strainer and allow to cool. The scum on the top of the stock will then set and should be removed.

Paella
Heat the olive oil in a paella pan and fry the onion, garlic and pepper until soft. Add the rice and turmeric, and fry for a further 3 minutes, turning constantly. Pour in 900ml/1½ pints of the chicken stock, season well and leave to cook over a moderate heat for 30 minutes, stirring occasionally. The rice will cook through and absorb the stock. If the pan becomes dry before the rice is completely cooked, add a little more stock.

At this point the paella could be left to cool and finished off just before serving.

About 15 minutes before you want to serve, make sure the pan is still moist with stock and stir in the chicken meat, sliced sausage, artichokes, tomato, mussels and squid. Arrange the king prawns around the circumference and place a lid on top. Cook like this for 10 minutes, then decorate with lemon wedges and parsley, and present the whole dish at the table.

Fresh Fruits with Manchego

The Spanish don't really go in for puddings, which provides a justifiable excuse not to bother. A basket of apricots, plums, cherries and strawberries, and, if you can find it, a piece of the strong Manchego sheep's cheese will make perfect authentic 'afters'.

Celebrating Summer

When there are no birthdays, anniversaries or other notable events in the diary worthy of celebration, why not celebrate the season itself? Here is a menu to do just that – freshly gathered wild mushrooms, a light fish main course and the yummiest summer pudding for years.

WARM MUSHROOM AND CAPER SALAD

....

SALMON TROUT AND PRAWN MONEYBAGS
WITH WATERCRESS CREAM SAUCE
NEW POTATOES
RUNNER BEANS

....

SUMMER PUDDING

WARM MUSHROOM AND CAPER SALAD

You have just walked back from the woods with a basket full of chanterelles, puffballs and cèpes, and you are about to create a little something 'sensational' (I know you have been to the supermarket really but not to worry).

🕐 20 minutes
Serves 6

150ml / ¼ pint olive oil
450g / 1lb large fresh woodland or field
  mushrooms, cut into pieces
2 garlic cloves, crushed
100g / 4oz jar of capers, drained
2 tbsp red wine vinegar
salt and freshly ground black pepper
1 curly endive
a few leaves of radicchio
1 round lettuce

Heat the olive oil in a frying pan and sauté the mushroom and garlic. Add the capers and vinegar, then season well with salt and pepper. Tear the lettuces into tufts and mix them on a serving platter. Spoon the hot mushroom mixture and juices over, and serve immediately.

SALMON TROUT AND PRAWN MONEYBAGS WITH WATERCRESS CREAM SAUCE

A golden 'moneybag' of filo pastry with a salmon and prawn filling, presented on a watercress sauce. A few new potatoes and some buttered runner beans would be a nice accompaniment.

🕐 1 hour, plus 25 and 20 minutes in the oven
Serves 6

1 (900g / 2lb) salmon trout
melted butter
450g / 1lb peeled prawns, drained
250ml / 8 fl oz crème fraîche
grated zest and juice of 1 lemon
salt and freshly ground black pepper
225g / 8oz filo pastry
1 bunch watercress
6 cooked langoustines to decorate

Preparation
Set the oven at 200°C/400°F/gas 6. Brush a sheet of foil with melted butter and wrap the salmon. Bake for 25 minutes. Skin the salmon and remove all the flesh from the bones. Mix with the prawns and 4 tbsp crème fraîche. Add the grated lemon zest (but not the juice) and season well.

Lay the filo pastry out on a work surface and cut into 20-cm/8-inch squares. Lay one square on top of another at an angle so you make an eight-pointed star. Place a large dollop of the fish mixture in the middle, brush a circle of water around it, then gather up all the sides and squeeze together at the top. Place the moneybags on an oiled baking sheet.

Put the remaining crème fraîche, lemon juice and more salt and pepper in a saucepan ready but don't make the sauce until just before serving. Set aside six sprigs of watercress and purée or chop the rest.

Cooking and serving
Set the oven at 170°C/325°F/gas 3. Bake the filo parcels for 20 minutes. Heat the crème fraîche mixture and, when hot, stir in the puréed or chopped watercress. Serve the parcels on individual plates with the sauce alongside, decorated with a sprig of watercress and a langoustine.

SUMMER PUDDING

There is nothing that can compete with a really good summer pudding and the myth that no-one can make it quite like your Granny used to is a load of old . . . fruit. The problems people encounter come from using under-ripe fresh berries which don't create enough juice. The modern way round this is to use some canned fruits along with the fresh.

🕐 25 minutes, plus 24 hours for compressing
Serves 6

450g / 1lb strawberries and/or raspberries, diced
450g / 1lb gooseberries or blackberries, cooked
1 (225g / 8oz) can blackcurrants
1 (225g / 8oz) can raspberries
about 3 tbsp caster sugar
¾ loaf thin-sliced bread, stale if possible
extra berries and mint leaves to decorate

Mix all the fruits in a sieve so the juice drains out into a bowl beneath. Sweeten the fruits to taste – the mixture wants to be tart but not 'cheek-sucking'.

You will need a 1.75-litre/3-pint pudding basin and the object now is to make a perfect bread lining to your basin. Cut the crusts off the bread and dip one side of each slice in the fruit juice before fitting it to the bowl (juice-side against the china). Lay a complete slice over the base and four complete slices up the sides, then cut triangles of bread to fit in the gaps. Now half-fill with fruit. Press it down well and place a **layer** of juice-dipped bread on top. Fill with the remainder of the fruit right up to the brim and again cover with a layer of bread.

Place a flat plate and some heavy weights on the top to press the pudding down. If you lack proper weights, some tins of baked beans will be ideal (don't pretend – I know you love them and have dozens in stock).

The pudding should be left in a cool place, weighted down, for 24 hours.

Remove the weights and plate, loosen the edges with a palette knife, place your serving dish upside-down over the pudding and turn both over together. Your 'perfect' summer pudding should then be decorated with mint leaves and fresh berries – just like Granny's.

Dip one side of each slice of bread into the fruit juice.

Lay a slice of bread over the base of the basin and four slices around the edges. Fill the gaps with triangles of bread.

59

Picnicking in the Countryside

One of the glorious British traditions is the outdoor feast, planned for a hot summer day and ending up with everyone crouched beneath dripping umbrellas. We cannot help our unpredictable climate but the picnic itself can be inspired whether it rains or the sun shines.

Let's try to avoid the inevitable soggy quiche and dry sandwiches. Here are some exciting and different dishes for you to try. In addition, I would always recommend a selection of interesting cheeses, French bread and plenty of ripe, fresh fruit.

DUCK TERRINE PARCELS WITH SOURED CREAM DIP
MINIATURE POTATO PIZZA SALAD
SMOKED SALMON AND CHIVE MOUSSE
DILL BLINIS WITH VARIOUS TOPPINGS

....

COFFEE MERINGUES WITH CLOTTED CREAM
SUMMER FRUIT TARTLETS

DUCK TERRINE PARCELS WITH SOURED CREAM DIP

This simple terrine, made in a food processor, takes only moments to prepare and tastes like *haute cuisine*! I wrap half in radicchio and half in young spinach leaves for a lovely two-colour presentation.

🕐 20 minutes
Makes about 20 parcels

2 (225g / 8oz) cooked or smoked duck breasts
25g / 1oz butter
50g / 2oz gherkins
50g / 2oz silverskin cocktail onions
1 tbsp sherry vinegar
2 tsp clear honey
salt and freshly ground black pepper
2 tsp pink peppercorns
100g / 4oz radicchio head
100g / 4oz large young spinach leaves

Soured Cream Dip
150ml / ¼ pint soured cream
75g / 3oz cream cheese
1 tbsp chopped fresh basil leaves

Cut one duck breast into fine dice. Chop the other breast roughly and blend in a food processor until smooth. Add the butter, gherkins, onions, sherry, honey and seasoning to the duck in the processor and blend again for a few seconds. Transfer the mixture to a bowl and stir in the diced duck and pink peppercorns.

Lay out individual radicchio and spinach leaves, and place a spoonful of the duck mixture on each. Roll the leaves into little parcels and arrange them on a dish.

For the soured cream dip, simply mix all the ingredients together and season to taste. Serve alongside the parcels.

MINIATURE POTATO PIZZA SALAD

Slices of new potato with a spicy pizza topping dotted among a crisp green salad. This unusual adaptation of pizza and salad proves popular with children and adults alike.

🕐 30 minutes
Serves 6–8

Potato Pizzas
6 large new potatoes, cooked
3 tbsp tomato purée
1 garlic clove, crushed
salt and freshly ground black pepper
a few drops of Tabasco
100g / 4oz Cheddar cheese, grated

Salad
1 frisée lettuce
a few leaves of lollo rosso
1 bunch radishes, quartered
vinaigrette dressing (page 46)

Slice the cooked potatoes into 6-mm/¼-inch thick discs. Mix the tomato purée with the garlic, season well, add a few drops of Tabasco and spread on the potato slices. Top with a generous layer of grated cheese and place under a hot grill until the cheese bubbles.

Tear the lettuce leaves roughly into a salad bowl. Arrange the potato pizzas randomly on top and then sprinkle the radishes over. Dress the salad with vinaigrette dressing just before serving.

SMOKED SALMON AND CHIVE MOUSSE

This will only be a disaster if the day of the picnic is so hot that your mousse becomes a smoked salmon and chive sauce. I shouldn't worry, however; if it's that hot, no-one will feel like eating anyway.

🕐 20 minutes, plus 2 hours for setting
Serves 8–10

225g / 8oz cooked salmon, canned or fresh
100g / 4oz smoked salmon pieces, chopped
300ml / ½ pint mayonnaise (see below)
1 tbsp lemon juice
1 tbsp sherry
1 tbsp snipped fresh chives
salt and freshly ground black pepper
3 tsp powdered gelatine
3 tbsp cold water
300ml / ½ pint double cream
chive flowers to decorate

Flake the cooked salmon and mix it with the smoked salmon pieces. Add the mayonnaise, lemon juice, sherry, chives and seasoning. Put the water in a small pan and sprinkle the gelatine over. Leave to one side for 3 minutes then place over a gentle heat and stir until the gelatine has dissolved. Mix the dissolved gelatine into the fish mixture. Whip the cream lightly and fold this into the mixture. Transfer the whole lot to a 1.1-litre/2-pint dish and leave to set. Decorate the top with a few chive flowers.

Mayonnaise

I keep putting mayonnaise in recipes but rather avoid the issue of making it. There is no beating the home-made variety (oh yes there is, excuse the pun) and, with the help of an electric whisk, it is really very simple.

🕐 10 minutes
Makes about 450ml / ¾ pint

2 egg yolks
1 tsp Dijon mustard
1 tbsp white wine vinegar
salt and freshly ground black pepper
300ml / ½ pint sunflower or groundnut oil

Beat the egg yolks, mustard and vinegar together and season well. Whisking continuously, start to add the oil very slowly – just a few drops at first, then a tablespoon at a time. It should take about 5 minutes of whisking before all the oil is incorporated and the mayonnaise is made.

What do we do with the whites? Read on for coffee meringues (page 63).

DILL BLINIS WITH VARIOUS TOPPINGS

To my mind, a home-made blini is infinitely more interesting than an ordinary open sandwich and its potential varieties are just as wide. The blinis can be made well in advance and may be frozen. The toppings, however, should be added on the day.

🕐 40 minutes, including toppings
Makes 20 × 6-cm / 2½-inch diameter blinis

100g / 4oz plain flour
1 tsp bicarbonate of soda
1 tsp cream of tartar
25g / 1oz caster sugar
1 egg
150ml / ¼ pint milk
2 tsp chopped fresh dill
oil for frying

Mix the flour, bicarbonate of soda, cream of tartar and sugar together. In a separate bowl, mix the egg and milk. Now whisk the egg and milk mixture into the dry ingredients until they are well blended. Add the chopped dill.

Heat a little oil in a heavy-based frying pan. However, you must wipe the oil off before cooking the blinis. Using a dessert spoon, spoon individual rounds of mixture on to the hot pan; only cook a few at a time. Cook for 1 minute; then, as the blinis bubble, turn them over with a palette knife and cook the other side briefly. Remove from the pan and leave to cool.

Spread the blinis with a little butter before topping them with any of the following mixtures.

Each tops 20 blinis

Salami and Mustard Seeds
575g / 1¼lb salami, thinly sliced
100g / 4oz soft cheese with herbs and garlic
2 tsp mustard seeds
50ml / 2 fl oz soured cream
fresh dill sprigs

Top each blini with sliced salami. Mix the herb cheese with the mustard seeds and soured cream, and dollop this on top. Decorate with a sprig of fresh dill.

Avocado with Orange
2 avocados, peeled and sliced
2 oranges, broken into segments
salt and freshly ground black pepper
lemon juice

Arrange the sliced avocado and the orange segments on each blini. Sprinkle with lemon juice and season with salt and pepper.

Prawn Mayonnaise with Apple
225g / 8oz peeled prawns, drained
4 tbsp mayonnaise (page 62)
1 green apple, quartered, cored and sliced
paprika
chopped parsley

Mix the prawns, mayonnaise and apple together and spoon on to each blini. Sprinkle a little paprika and chopped parsley on top.

COFFEE MERINGUE WITH CLOTTED CREAM

Meringues with the nutty aroma of freshly ground coffee served with lashings of clotted cream.

🕐 15 minutes, plus 1½ hours in the oven
Makes 16

3 egg whites
175g / 6oz soft brown sugar
2 tsp freshly ground coffee beans
150ml / ¼ pint clotted cream

Set the oven at 110°C/225°F/gas ¼. Line a baking sheet with baking parchment.

Whisk the egg whites until very stiff. Continue whisking while adding the sugar a tablespoon at a time, allowing the sugar to mix in well between spoonfuls. Finally whisk in the ground coffee.

Pipe the meringue mixture in small rosettes on to the baking parchment. Bake for 1½ hours. Take the meringues to your picnic in an airtight container and serve with the clotted cream.

SUMMER FRUIT TARTLETS

Please don't be put off by the fiddly mini pastry cases and the three stages for making these. They are so pretty and will be so much admired at your picnic, I promise it is worth the effort.

🕐 1 hour, plus 10 minutes in the oven
Makes 12

350g / 12oz frozen puff pastry, thawed
(I would not dream of asking you to make the pastry)

Crème Patissière
50g / 2oz caster sugar
3 egg yolks
25g / 1oz plain flour
pinch of salt
250ml / 8 fl oz milk
1 tsp vanilla essence

Fruits and Glaze
450g / 1lb (total weight) mixed fresh fruit and berries such as apricots and redcurrants, or raspberries and blueberries, or green grapes and cherries
3 tbsp apricot jam

Pastry Cases
Set the oven at 200°C/400°F/gas 6 and oil a 7.5-cm/3-inch tartlet sheet.

Roll out the puff pastry very thinly (less than 3mm/⅛ inch thick). With a crinkly-edged pastry cutter cut 10-cm/4-inch rounds and fit these into the tartlet moulds (the pastry is deliberately a size larger than the moulds). Use a fork to prick the base of each pastry case several times.

Bake the tartlets for 5 minutes, then look at the disaster you have created. The pastry will have puffed up and will bear no resemblance to individual tartlet cases. Don't despair: use the end of a 5-cm/2-inch diameter rolling pin to 'stamp' down each pastry case back into its mould. Return the pastry to the oven and cook for a further 5 minutes. (That may sound like the most 'Heath Robinson' recipe you have ever heard but it really is most effective.)

Crème Patissière
Whisk the sugar and egg yolks together in a bowl until thick and creamy, then work in the flour and salt. Heat the milk and vanilla essence in a heavy-based pan and bring to the boil. As the mixture boils up in the pan, pour into the bowl of egg mixture, stirring continuously. Now tip the whole mixture back into the pan. Place over a very gentle heat and stir continuously until the custard comes to the boil and thickens. Leave to cool.

Assembling the Tartlets
Put a spoonful of crème pat (as it's called in the trade) in the base of each tartlet case. Choose different combinations of your favourite summer fruits and berries. Arrange these on top of the custard. Heat the apricot jam in a small saucepan, pass it through a sieve and brush on to the top of each tart. Allow the glaze to cool and set.

Well Ahead of the Jones's

What's the point in just keeping up, when you could be way out in front? Once in a while I am sure it's all right to show off a little bit and this particular menu really will be the talk of the hairdressers – how can I be so rude?

ICED APPLE AND MINT SOUP

....

BALLOTTINE OF THREE FILLETS
WITH MUSTARD BEARNAISE SAUCE
VEGETABLE BUNDLES

....

ALMOND CREME BRULEE
WITH RASPBERRIES AND BLUEBERRIES

ICED APPLE AND
MINT SOUP

I can smell the newly mown grass and feel the warmth of the evening sun as I look at this recipe – just you wait until you taste it.

🕐 35 minutes, plus 2 hours for chilling
Serves 6

6 Cox's apples
small bunch fresh mint
1 medium onion, finely chopped
1.75 litres / 3 pints chicken stock
75g / 3oz butter
75g / 3oz plain flour
salt and freshly ground black pepper
150ml / ¼ pint double cream

Peel, core and roughly chop the apples. Set aside six mint leaves and finely chop the rest.

Heat the chicken stock in a large pan and cook the apples and onion in it for 20 minutes. Transfer the mixture to a food processor and blend until smooth.

Melt the butter in a large saucepan, stir in the flour and cook for 1 minute. Add the apple mixture slowly, stirring continuously, until the soup is smooth and comes to the boil. Remove from the heat. Season well with salt and pepper. Stir in the cream and chopped mint; leave to cool and then chill well.

Serve in individual dishes with a fresh mint leaf to decorate.

BALLOTTINE OF THREE FILLETS
WITH MUSTARD BEARNAISE SAUCE

Fillets of beef, lamb and pork with mushroom pâté encased in bacon and served with a mustard béarnaise sauce; although one of the most 'over-the-top' recipes in this book, taken step by step, the making is quite easy and the results magnificent.

Take care choosing the three fillets – each one needs to be of an even thickness and similar in length (about 18–20cm/7–8 inches).

🕐 1 hour, plus 25 minutes and 25 minutes in the oven
Serves 6

450g / 1lb thin tail end of fillet of beef,
*   trimmed*
450g / 1lb loin of lamb, with all the fat
*   trimmed off, leaving just the eye of the*
*   meat*
350g / 12oz pork tenderloin, trimmed
175g / 6oz mushrooms, finely chopped
1 onion, finely chopped
25g / 1oz margarine
salt and freshly ground black pepper
1 garlic clove, crushed
2 tbsp chopped parsley
450g / 1lb streaky bacon, rinds removed
flat-leafed parsley and nasturtium flower
*   (optional) to decorate*
mustard béarnaise sauce (see below)

Preparation
Set the oven at 220°C/425°F/gas 7.

We begin by part-cooking the meats before the dish is assembled: roast the lamb fillet for 10 minutes, the beef for 15 minutes and the pork for 25 minutes. That sounds more complicated than it is. They all go in together in one tin and you just lift each fillet out on time and leave to cool. Save the juices.

Prepare the mushroom pâté by first melting the margarine in a frying pan, then adding the mushrooms, onion and garlic. Cook for 5 minutes, season well, stir in the chopped parsley and leave to cool.

Stretch out the strips of bacon to at least 25cm/10 inches long and lay them parallel, flat on the work surface, each one slightly overlapping the next until you have a square sheet of bacon 25 × 25cm/10 × 10 inches. Lay the lamb and the pork fillets together across the bacon strips. Spread the pâté on to the meats and lay the beef fillet on top. Now carefully fold the bacon over the meats from both sides, making a complete parcel. Roll the whole parcel over so the bacon joint is on the underside and transfer to an oiled tin ready to roast.

Final cooking and serving
Set the oven at 200°C/400°F/gas 6.

Roast the ballottine for 25 minutes and allow it to 'rest' before carving. Slice 2-cm/ ¾-inch pieces across the three fillets, decorate with a sprig of flat-leafed parsley and, if possible, a nasturtium flower. Serve with mustard béarnaise sauce (below).

Mustard Béarnaise Sauce
Makes about 300ml / ½ pint
300ml / ½ pint hollandaise sauce (page 28)
2 tsp fresh chopped chives
2 tsp fresh chopped tarragon
2 tsp chopped parsley
1 tbsp Dijon mustard
meat juices

Prepare the sauce by mixing the basic hollandaise with the herbs, mustard and the meat juices from the first cooking. Leave the sauce in a warm place so it can be served tepid.

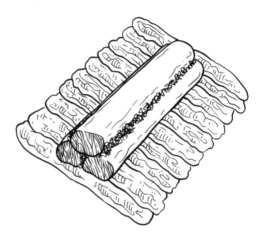

Lay the lamb and pork fillets across the overlapping bacon strips, spread the pâté on the meats and place the beef fillet on top.

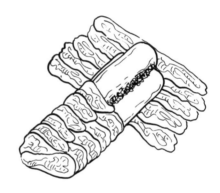

Fold the bacon strips carefully over the meats to make a parcel.

VEGETABLE BUNDLES

Individual bundles of baby vegetables tied together with a band of leek.

🕐 30 minutes, including cooking
Serves 6

12 baby carrots
18 thin asparagus spears, trimmed to a
*   length of 13cm / 5 inches*
12 baby sweetcorn
2 leeks, cut lengthways into long strips
melted butter

Preparation
Cook the carrots, asparagus and sweetcorn separately by plunging each vegetable into boiling salted water, cooking until tender, then scooping them out and immediately refreshing under the cold tap. Do the same for the strips of leek but literally cook for just 1 minute.

Arrange the vegetables in bundles of two carrots, three asparagus spears and two sweetcorn. Tie each bundle with a double strip of leek. Place the vegetables on a buttered baking sheet and brush melted butter all over. Cover with a layer of greaseproof paper and foil.

Final cooking and serving
Set the oven at 220°C/425°F/gas 7.

Just 5 minutes before serving the main course, place the vegetables in the oven. Once hot, serve immediately alongside the Ballotine.

ALMOND CREME BRULEE WITH RASPBERRIES AND BLUEBERRIES

Crème brûlée with fresh berries is my ultimate summer dessert – so much so that it is wasted on the Jones's, on second thoughts, therefore, let's not invite them at all.

🕐 15 minutes, plus 1½ hours in the oven
Serves 6

8 egg yolks
175g / 6oz caster sugar
2 tbsp Amaretto liqueur (if unavailable, a
*   few drops of almond essence would do)*
600ml / 1 pint single cream
100g / 4oz demerara sugar
450g / 1lb raspberries
225g / 8oz blueberries

Set the oven at 160°C/325°F/gas 3 and butter a 1.1-litre/2-pint soufflé dish.

Blend together the egg yolks, caster sugar and almond liqueur with a wooden spoon (have a quick swig of the liqueur on its own – it's divine). Heat the cream in a saucepan until almost boiling and pour it over the egg and sugar, stirring while you do so.

Transfer the mixture to the soufflé dish and stand it in a roasting tin. Pour as much cold water as you can into the tin and then bake for 1½ hours. Remove the dish from the tin and leave to cool.

Set the grill at high. Spread a generous layer of demerara sugar on top of the crème and place it under the grill until the sugar almost burns. Chill again, before serving alongside a bowl of raspberries and blueberries.

Light that Barbie!

That's not just a trendy 'down under' slogan to herald this section on outdoor cooking; it is actually the best advice I can give. The tendency is to light the fire far too late and find it is perfect for cooking about an hour after your last guests went home. In the meantime you have been struggling either to blow the fire into life or to douse your flaming meats with buckets of water. Take heed – light a good-sized fire early on and cook on red glowing embers.

Now, what shall we cook? The most basic sausage or hamburger is much more exciting done on the barbecue and as for a few king prawns or shrimps – yummy. But let me give you some ideas for more unusual dishes which even those from 'down under' may not have sampled.

BROCHETTES OF CHICKEN AND MANGO
LOIN OF LAMB WITH LEEK AND MARJORAM STUFFING
GARLIC SQUID
SWORDFISH STEAKS MARINATED IN DILL AND LIME
STUFFED RED AND GREEN PEPPERS

BROCHETTES OF CHICKEN AND MANGO

Spicy pieces of chicken breast with the sweet, oily flavour of mango, served on a bed of green rocket or lamb's lettuce lightly dressed with oil and lemon juice.

🕐 15 minutes, plus 1 hour for marinating and 15 minutes for barbecuing
Makes 12 brochettes

3 mangoes
1 tbsp lemon juice
1 tsp chilli sauce
1 tbsp groundnut or sunflower oil
1 tsp English mustard
salt
3 (225g / 8oz) chicken breasts, cut in
*   2.5-cm/1-inch cubes*

Peel the mangoes and cut the flesh away from the stones into small chunks; do this over a bowl so that all the juices are saved. Add the lemon juice, chilli sauce, oil, mustard and salt to the mango juices, then roll the chicken cubes and mango flesh in the mixture. Leave to marinate for at least 1 hour.

Skewer the pieces of chicken and mango alternately on to 12 wooden brochette sticks. Cook the brochettes on the edges of the barbecue for 10–15 minutes, turning frequently.

LOIN OF LAMB WITH LEEK AND MARJORAM STUFFING

For some reason, cooking a whole joint of meat on the barbecue is considered far more challenging than grilling individual pieces. One could say, however, there is far less to go wrong – you only have one thing to burn or serve raw instead of half a dozen. Let's see if we can get it right.

🕐 30 minutes, plus 40 minutes for barbecuing
Serves 6

1 (900g–1.5kg / 2–3lb) boned and rolled
*   loin of lamb*

Stuffing
350g / 12oz leeks, thinly sliced
25g / 1oz margarine
2 tbsp soft breadcrumbs
1 tbsp raisins
1 tbsp fresh marjoram leaves
salt and freshly ground black pepper

Preparation
The butcher will have tied the loin up beautifully with a series of little strings. You will have to cut these in order to unroll the meat for stuffing.

To prepare the stuffing, fry the leeks in the margarine until they are soft and tender. Stir in the breadcrumbs, raisins and marjoram, and season well with salt and pepper.

Place an even strip of the stuffing along the length of the unrolled loin. Now re-roll the meat and tie it as neatly and tightly as possible.

Cooking and serving
The lamb will cook in about 40 minutes over a hot fire. Place the loin in the centre of the grill and roll it frequently in order to seal

all round the outside. Douse the fire with a water spray if it flares up. Once the lamb is scorched all over, cover it with a lid of some sort (an upside-down roasting tin or sheet of foil would do) in order to hold the heat into the centre of the meat. Cook like this for about 30 minutes, turning occasionally. Transfer the cooked lamb to a carving board, slice and serve.

GARLIC SQUID

Char-grilled squid is one of my very favourite dishes but beware – only moments after it is tender and delicious, it will become tasteless and rubbery if left on the fire too long.

🕐 10 minutes, plus 1 hour for marinating – plus instant cooking!
Serves 6

675g / 1½lb baby squid, cleaned and
  prepared
3 tbsp olive oil
2 garlic cloves, crushed
salt and freshly ground black pepper
2 lemons, cut into wedges

Preparation
Heat a pan of water to boiling point and plunge the squid into it for just 10 seconds. Drain and allow to cool. Mix the oil with garlic and season well. Brush this mixture on to the squid and leave to marinate for at least 1 hour.

Cooking and serving
Grill the squid on a hot fire for 1 minute each side. Transfer to a serving platter, pour

any remaining oil and garlic over and decorate with lemon wedges.

My birthday is in June – I can't wait.

SWORDFISH STEAKS MARINATED IN DILL AND LIME

This dish requires a rather timid and smoky fire so that the fish is warm-smoked rather than grilled. Try adding some newly cut apple wood to the charcoal.

🕐 10 minutes, plus 3 hours for marinating and 15 minutes barbecuing
Serves 6

6 (175g / 6oz) swordfish steaks
lime wedges

Marinade
grated zest and juice of 2 limes
1 tbsp chopped fresh dill
2 tsp pink peppercorns
2 tsp caster sugar
2 tbsp oil
salt and freshly ground black pepper

Arrange the swordfish in a shallow dish. Mix all the ingredients for the marinade together and pour over. Leave to 'brew' for 2–3 hours.

Grill the fish over a gentle heat for 10 minutes on one side, then 5 or 6 minutes on the other, occasionally spooning the marinade over while it cooks. Serve with wedges of lime and some colourful salads.

71

STUFFED RED AND GREEN PEPPERS

These make a lovely alternative to meats cooked on the barbecue and are one of the few vegetables that really takes the flavour of the fire. I would serve them with new potatoes and a home-made tomato sauce.

🕐 1 hour, including barbecuing
Serves 6

3 red peppers
3 green peppers
3 tbsp olive oil
2 small red onions, chopped
2 garlic cloves, crushed
2 tbsp pine kernels
100g / 4oz lentils, cooked
1 tbsp chopped parsley
salt and freshly ground black pepper
olive oil for cooking
*extra parsley and green salad leaves to
    decorate*

Preparation
Cut the peppers in two lengthways, including the stalks. Scoop out the pips and inner core.

Heat the oil in a pan and fry the onion, garlic and pine kernels together for 5 minutes. Remove from the heat, mix in the lentils and parsley and season with salt and pepper. Spoon this mixture into the pepper halves and sandwich them back together.

Cooking and serving
Brush the peppers with oil and roast them over a moderate fire, turning occasionally, until they are soft and tender.

Re-split the two halves and arrange one red and one green half-pepper on individual plates. Decorate with chopped parsley and green salad leaves.

Autumn Fruit and Nut Flan
Spiced Pears with Blue Wensleydale
Wild Mushroom and Aubergine Gougère
Selection of brunch dishes

ENTERTAINING IN THE
Autumn

There is a special smell to autumn which harmonizes perfectly with the colours changing to reds and browns, the gathering of nuts, ripening of plums, windy walks and returning home to light the first fire.

When the mushroom season finishes and the game season begins is the best culinary time of year. Wholesome soups, mellow stews and rustic pies can contrast with quantities of blackberries, apples, pears and the last of the summer salads.

Any excuse will do to serve this marvellous food – celebrate the harvest or the downfall of dear old Guy Fawkes. A hot buffet lunch or a dinner party to impress the Chairman.

The Chairman to Dinner

Somehow the Chairman has been invited to dinner. What on earth are you going to serve and what will he think?

The spiced pears with cheese will show you to be subtle and creative: 'Clearly an asset to the firm.' The fish main course demonstrates healthy living and style without going over-budget: 'This person will go far.' And the syllabub indicates an ability to indulge a little: 'Never trust a saint.'

Now don't foul up on the coffee.

Spiced Pears with Blue Wensleydale

....

Rondelles of Plaice Wrapped in Cabbage Leaves with Tarragon Butter Sauce
Autumn Vegetables

....

Madeira and Lemon Syllabub

SPICED PEARS WITH BLUE WENSLEYDALE

A savoury spiced pear with mild blue cheese and a little leafy salad alongside.

🕐 40 minutes, including cooking
Serves 6

3 firm (nice-shaped) pears such as William
175ml / 6 fl oz cider vinegar
100ml / 4 fl oz cold water
100g / 4oz caster sugar
2 tbsp lemon juice
2 tbsp pink peppercorns
1 tsp whole cloves
1 tsp ground mace
1 cinnamon stick
350g / 12oz blue Wensleydale cheese, sliced
    into 12
1 curly endive, washed and broken into tufts
a few leaves of radicchio and oak leaf
    lettuce, washed and broken into tufts

I find it easier to peel the pears whole and then halve them but, either way, you need peeled, halved pears with their stalks on and the cores scooped out.

In a medium-sized saucepan heat the vinegar, water, sugar, lemon juice and spices; bring to the boil. Add the pears and poach them until soft. Remove the pear halves from the liquid and allow to cool. Fan the pears by carefully making a series of parallel cuts, leaving the top of each slice attached. Gosh, that sounds complicated – have a look at the drawing, it may help.

Place a pear half on each plate and press down so it fans out. Arrange two slices of cheese alongside and add a little mound of the salad. Dress the pear and salad with the cooking liquid, making sure the colourful spices are dotted over evenly.

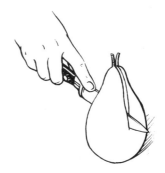

Peel and halve the pears keeping the stalks on.

Make a series of parallel cuts.

RONDELLES OF PLAICE WRAPPED IN CABBAGE LEAVES WITH TARRAGON BUTTER SAUCE

Now this is a little gem – as easy as anything but with an end result which will look as though it has jumped off the front cover of a glossy magazine. Catherine wheels of white fish interleaved with green and orange set on a tarragon butter sauce.

🕐 35 minutes, plus 15 minutes in the oven
Serves 6

75

1 Savoy cabbage
6 carrots
6 (175g / 6oz) plaice fillets
salt and freshly ground black pepper
chopped fresh tarragon
flat-leafed parsley to decorate
tarragon butter sauce (see below)

Preparation

Break six large leaves away from the cabbage and blanch them in boiling water for 30 seconds. Drain and refresh under the cold tap. Peel the carrots, cut each into five or six strips and cook in boiling water for 5 minutes. Drain and refresh as you did the cabbage.

Cut the thick part of the stalk out of the cabbage leaves and lay the leaves out on the work surface. Lay a fillet of plaice on top of each leaf. Season the fish with salt and pepper and sprinkle with chopped tarragon. Place five strips of carrot across the fish. Now roll the whole thing into a tight log. (If you have ever been inside a tight log, you will know exactly what I am talking about!) transfer to a buttered roasting tin and cover with buttered greaseproof paper and foil.

Cooking and serving

Set the oven at 200°C/400°F/gas 6.

Bake the fish for 15 minutes. Transfer to a chopping board and carve each into three slices. Arrange three slices on each plate cut-side up to resemble a clover leaf. Pour tarragon butter sauce around the fish and decorate with a sprig of flat-leafed parsley. Serve immediately with some simple autumn vegetables.

Tarragon Butter Sauce

Not good for the waistline but great for the taste-buds.

🕐 10 minutes
Makes about 450ml / ¾ pint

175ml / 6 fl oz thick crème fraîche
4 tbsp tarragon vinegar
1 tbsp caster sugar
1 tsp salt
freshly ground black pepper
175g / 6oz butter, cut in small pieces

In a small pan heat the crème fraîche, tarragon vinegar, sugar, salt and pepper. When the mixture is hot but not boiling, remove from the heat and whisk in the butter. Keep whisking until the mixture is completely smooth. The sauce should be served warm and, if made in advance, can be gently re-heated in a bowl over a pan of hot water.

MADEIRA AND LEMON SYLLABUB

Incredibly simple and quite irresistible (now that's no way to talk about my wife!).

🕐 5–10 minutes
Serves 6

300ml / ½ pint double cream
75g / 3oz caster sugar
grated zest and juice of 1 large lemon
4 tbsp Madeira (if unavailable, sherry will do)
50g / 2oz flaked almonds, toasted under the grill

Put all the ingredients except the almonds in a large bowl and whip with an electric mixer to a firm folding consistency: be careful not to over-whip. Transfer to a serving dish and sprinkle the top with the toasted almonds to decorate.

Too Many to Sit Down

There are those occasions when the guest list steadily expands until you cannot possibly seat everyone. The answer is to produce a hot fork buffet laid out on the kitchen table and just let guests fend for themselves. But rather than the stringy chicken casserole and soggy trifle that are traditional to these occasions, why not prepare some more original dishes? This buffet has a choice of a meat or fish main course, but I bet most people will try both.

DUCK WITH APPLE AND CALVADOS

....

MACKEREL AND ALMOND CROQUETTES
WITH RED CABBAGE
SAVOYARDE POTATOES

....

SPICED FROMAGE FRAIS WITH PLUM AND ORANGE
AUTUMN FRUIT AND NUT FLAN

Duck with Apple and Calvados

Although I am suggesting this dish for a buffet, it is equally suitable as a dinner party main course . . . slices of duck breast, cooked in cider, decorated with balls of apple in a rich Calvados sauce.

🕐 1 hour, including 30 minutes in the oven
Serves 6–8

4 (225g / 8oz) duck breasts
25g / 1oz margarine
600ml / 1 pint cider
150ml / ¼ pint apple juice (from a carton)
2 tbsp lemon juice
1 chicken stock cube, crumbled
2 tsp light brown sugar
50g / 2oz plain flour
3 tbsp Calvados
2 tbsp crème fraîche
salt and freshly ground black pepper
3 Cox's apples
chopped parsley

Preparation
Set the oven at 200°C/400°F/gas 6.

Melt the margarine in a large frying pan and cook the duck breasts until they are golden brown on both sides. Transfer them to a roasting tin, skin-side up.

Pour the cider, apple and lemon juice over the duck and add the stock cube and sugar. Bake, uncovered, for 30 minutes. Once cooked, remove the duck from the cooking liquid and leave it to cool.

Now to make the sauce: re-heat the cooking fat and stir in the flour. Allow to cook for a minute, then gradually stir in all the duck cooking liquid. When the sauce is thick and smooth, add the Calvados and crème fraîche. Season to taste. Leave the sauce to cool until needed.

Halve the apples and, using a 'baller', scoop rounds of apple flesh out of each half. Add these to the pan of sauce. Carve the cold duck breasts into 3-mm/⅛-inch thick slices and keep chilled until required.

Final cooking and serving
Re-heat the sauce gently, stirring occasionally until it comes to the boil. Add the sliced duck breast, allow the sauce to boil again and then transfer to a serving dish. Sprinkle with chopped parsley.

Mackerel and Almond Croquettes with Red Cabbage

I have chosen to use mackerel, although many other varieties of flavoursome fish could be substituted for this almond-coated fishcake.

🕐 1¼ hours, including oven-cooking
Serves 6–8

625g / 1½lb mackerel
butter for cooking fish
450g / 1lb potatoes, cooked and mashed
2 tbsp plain yoghurt
4 tsp grated horseradish
25g / 1oz butter
salt and freshly ground black pepper
175g / 6oz almonds, chopped
oil for frying

Red Cabbage
1 small red cabbage
1 small onion, finely diced
25g / 1oz margarine
2 tbsp redcurrant jelly
2 tbsp red wine vinegar
salt and freshly ground black pepper
snipped fresh chives to decorate
125ml / 4 fl oz soured cream

Preparation

Set the oven at 200°C/400°F/gas 6.

Place the mackerel in a well-buttered ovenproof dish and bake for 20 minutes. Allow to cool.

Remove the fish skin and fillet the flesh carefully, avoiding any bones. In a large mixing bowl, blend together the mackerel flesh, mashed potato, yoghurt and horseradish. Melt the butter in a small pan and blend this into the mixture. Season well. Now, take tablespoonfuls of the croquette mixture and roll them into even rounds between the palms of your hands (just like playing with plasticine). Spread the chopped almonds on a flat plate and roll each round in the almonds until well-coated. Chill the croquettes in the refrigerator before frying.

Heat a deep pan of oil and fry the croquettes for about 5 minutes until golden-brown. Remove them from the oil and place on a tin, ready to re-heat when needed.

To prepare the red cabbage, core and shred the cabbage finely. Cook in boiling, salted water for 10 minutes until the cabbage is softened but still crisp. Drain and then refresh the cabbage by running cold water through it. Melt the margarine in a pan and fry the onion in it. Add the cabbage and stir in the redcurrant jelly, vinegar, salt and pepper. Sauté the mixture for 10 minutes. Transfer to an ovenproof serving dish, lid on, ready to heat up when required.

Final cooking and serving

Put the cabbage in the oven 20 minutes before it is required and then, 10 minutes later, put in the fish croquettes. Once they are both hot, arrange the fish on top of the cabbage and sprinkle with the chives. Serve a bowl of soured cream alongside. Tomato and Mangetout Vinaigrette (see page 83) would be a nice accompaniment, if you want to serve a salad.

SAVOYARDE POTATOES

I have a passion for sliced, baked potatoes and they can be made in all sorts of different ways, each with its own fancy French name. Dauphinois is made with a milky scrambled egg mixture and lots of nutmeg; boulangère has onion and stock; and Savoyarde (my favourite) is cooked with Gruyère cheese, garlic and stock.

🕐 10 minutes, plus 1½ hours in the oven
Serves 8–10

*1.25 kg / 2½ lb old potatoes, peeled and
    thinly sliced*
225g / 8oz Gruyère cheese, grated
*600ml / 1 pint chicken stock (water and a
    stock cube will do)*
3 garlic cloves, crushed
salt and freshly ground black pepper

Set the oven at 180°C/350°F/gas 4.

In an ovenproof dish, layer half the sliced potatoes and sprinkle over half the cheese. Layer the remaining potatoes and cheese on top. Heat the chicken stock with the garlic and season well. Pour the stock into the dish of potatoes and bake, uncovered, for 1½ hours.

SPICED FROMAGE FRAIS WITH PLUM AND ORANGE

A delightfully simple, low-fat dessert comprising a layer of spiced and slightly sweetened fromage frais covered with a layer of fresh fruit.

🕐 15 minutes
Serves 6

600ml / 1 pint low-fat fromage frais
2 tbsp caster sugar
1 tsp ground cinnamon
1 tsp grated nutmeg
½ tsp ground cloves
3 oranges
450g / 1lb ripe red plums
1 tbsp brown sugar crystals

Mix the fromage frais with the sugar and spices, then grate the orange zest into the mixture. Peel the oranges and cut the flesh out of each segment, discarding all the pith. Halve, de-stone and segment the plums. Spread the spiced fromage frais in the bottom of a shallow serving dish, randomly arrange the two fruits on top and sprinkle with the brown sugar crystals.

AUTUMN
FRUIT AND NUT FLAN

This stunning-looking flan requires a fair degree of care and attention but is well worth the effort.

🕐 50 minutes, plus 20 minutes in the oven
Serves 6–8

Rich Almond Pastry
175g / 6oz plain flour
50g / 2oz ground almonds
2 tbsp caster sugar
¼ tsp salt
100g / 4oz butter, cut into knobs
50g / 2oz lard, cut into knobs
2 egg yolks
2 tbsp cold water

Filling and Glaze
2 Cox's apples, peeled, cored and sliced
100g / 4oz black grapes, halved and pipped
100g / 4oz white grapes, halved and pipped
100g / 4oz dried apricots, halved
50g / 2oz walnuts, shelled in halves
3 tbsp brandy
2 tbsp clear honey
3 tbsp apricot jam

Set the oven at 200°C/400°F/gas 6. Oil a 20-cm/8-inch flan tin.

Mix the flour, ground almonds, sugar and salt together. Rub the butter and lard into the flour mixture with your fingertips. Mix the egg yolks and water together; pour into a 'well' in the flour mixture and knead the whole thing together. (This must be done as swiftly as possible and should end up soft – not sticky. Roll the pastry out on a floured surface and then fit it carefully into the flan tin, pinching off any excess around the edge. Prick the base of the pastry all over with a fork.

Now, the mystery of baking 'blind'. Crumple a sheet of greaseproof paper so it will fit into the pastry case and fill it with uncooked rice to prevent the pastry from rising off the base of the tin. Bake the case for 10 minutes, then remove the greaseproof and rice. Return the pastry to the oven for 10 minutes.

Now the filling. Dice half the fruit and nuts finely and heat them in a pan with brandy and honey. Once the apple has softened, spoon this mixture into the cooked pastry case. Now, arrange the other half of the filling ingredients in neat parallel lines across the top of the flan; a row of sliced apple, a row of walnut halves, and so on. Return the flan to the oven and bake for 10 minutes.

Finally, melt the apricot jam in a small pan and pass it through a sieve. Brush this glaze over the flan and leave to cool and set.

Indian Summer (or is it Alaskan?)

No, this has nothing to do with a curry take-away down the road run by an Alaskan. It's a time for golden sunsets, harvest moons, a few lovely warm days in late September and the last opportunity for a meal in the garden.

WARM BACON AND GOAT'S CHEESE SALAD

....

WILD MUSHROOM AND AUBERGINE GOUGERE
TOMATO AND MANGETOUT VINAIGRETTE

....

BAKED ALASKA WITH CASSIS SAUCE

WARM BACON AND GOAT'S CHEESE SALAD

'mmm – I can taste it now!

🕐 15 minutes, plus 10 minutes in the oven
Serves 6

½ loaf of small-diameter French bread
200ml / 7 fl oz olive oil
3 garlic cloves, crushed
175g / 6oz goat's cheese
175g / 6 oz streaky bacon rashers, rinds
  removed
1 oak leaf lettuce
1 punnet lamb's tongue salad
a few leaves of radicchio
3 tbsp walnut oil
salt and freshly ground black pepper
2 tbsp red wine vinegar

Set the oven at 180°C/350°F/gas 4.

Cut the French bread into 1-cm/½-inch thick slices. Mix the olive oil with garlic and brush some on to each slice, keeping the remainder for the dressing. Slice or spread the goat's cheese on to each piece of bread. Transfer these to a baking sheet and bake for 10 minutes.

Use a little more of the olive oil to fry the bacon until it is crispy; cut it into small pieces and keep warm. Tear the lettuces into small tufts and arrange them in a serving dish.

In a small pan, heat the remaining garlicky olive and the walnut oil and season well. Remove from the heat and add the red wine vinegar.

Arrange the goat's cheese croûtes across the salad and sprinkle the bacon on top. Spoon over the hot dressing and serve.

WILD MUSHROOM AND AUBERGINE GOUGERE

Savoury choux pastry with a rich mushroom filling that will bring the smells of deep rural France into your kitchen. The dried wild mushrooms are expensive and, of course, not essential but, if you can get hold of them, they really will make all the difference.

🕐 45 minutes, plus 4 hours for soaking and 30 minutes in the oven
Serves 6

Mushroom Filling
50g / 2oz dried wild mushrooms
150ml / ¼ pint milk
50g / 2oz margarine
350g / 12oz field mushrooms, sliced
1 young aubergine, chopped
25g / 1oz plain flour
125ml / 4 fl oz red wine
2 garlic cloves, crushed
a few drops of Worcestershire sauce
salt and freshly ground black pepper
2 tbsp black treacle

Choux Pastry
150ml / ¼ pint water
50g / 2oz butter
65g / 2½oz plain flour
2 eggs
50g / 2oz gruyère cheese, grated
cayenne pepper
salt
chopped parsley to decorate

Mushroom filling
Soak the dried mushrooms in milk for a good 4 hours before use. Melt the margarine in a large frying pan and sauté the field mushrooms and aubergine until they are soft. Sprinkle over the flour and stir it in.

Now, stir in the dried mushrooms with their milk, the red wine, garlic, Worcestershire sauce, seasoning and black treacle. Yes, black treacle – it darkens, sweetens and enriches all in one go, ah . . . Allow the mixture to cook for a few minutes, then move it off the heat.

Choux pastry

Boil the water and butter together until they bubble up the pan. Remove the pan from the heat and immediately add all the flour in one go. Beat the mixture until quite smooth. Return to the heat and allow to cook for about 2 minutes, then beat in the eggs. Continue to beat for 2–3 minutes, then add the cheese and season well. Spoon the mixture around the edge of a buttered ovenproof dish, making a complete ring. Spoon the mushroom filling into the centre.

Spoon the mixture around the edge of an oven-proof dish, using one spoon to scrape the mixture off the other.

(You can leave this uncooked for up to 2 hours, if required.)

Cooking and serving

Set the oven at 200°C/400°F/gas 6.

Bake the gougère for 30 minutes, sprinkle chopped parsley over the top and serve. Florets of broccoli make an attractive accompaniment.

TOMATO AND MANGETOUT VINAIGRETTE

A simple, colourful salad to complement either fish or meat.

⊕ 10 minutes
Serves 8–10

225g / 8oz mangetout, topped and tailed
10 medium tomatoes
vinaigrette dressing (page 46)
chopped fresh dill

Plunge the mangetout into a pan of boiling salted water. Cook for 1 minute, then drain and immediately refresh under the cold tap.

Slice the tomatoes, arrange with the mangetout on a serving dish and dress with vinaigrette dressing and chopped dill.

BAKED ALASKA WITH
CASSIS SAUCE

Surely, I hear you say, in a book that professes to make cookery for entertaining easy, a Baked Alaska is the most difficult dessert even to consider serving. Italian restaurants have been living off that myth for years, serving Alaska as a special birthday treat which commands exorbitant prices and appreciative tips. We are about to spoil all that – there are just three elements: a good home-made ice-cream, stiff meringue and nerve – when you place the whole thing in a very hot oven and pray.

🕐 20 minutes, plus 12 hours for freezing and 4 minutes in the oven
Serves 6–8

Ice-cream
6 egg yolks
225g / 8oz caster sugar
grated zest and juice of 2 lemons
300ml / ½ pint double cream

Meringue
4 egg whites
225g / 8oz caster sugar

Cassis Sauce
450g / 1lb canned blackcurrants

Ice-cream
Put the yolks and sugar in an electric mixer and beat them until they double in volume and turn pale in colour. Heat the lemon juice and zest in a small pan. As it comes to the boil, pour it into the egg and sugar mixture and continue to heat for another minute. Whip the cream in a separate bowl until it is stiff enough to 'leave a trace'. Fold the cream into the mixture and pour the whole thing into a 1.1-litre/2-pint pudding basin.

Leave in the freezer for at least 12 hours, then dip the basin in hot water and turn the ice-cream out on to a serving dish. Return the turned-out ice-cream to the freezer.

Meringue
Whisk the whites until very stiff. Continue whisking while adding the caster sugar very gradually – a little at a time. Once all the sugar is blended in, take the ice-cream from the freezer and spoon a generous layer of meringue all over it. Shape it with a palette knife but don't try to be too neat – lots of Alaskan peaks. Return the whole thing to the freezer until 'the moment'.

Cassis sauce
Simply purée the canned blackcurrants and then put the purée through a sieve to remove the seeds. Dilute with a little water if the sauce is too thick.

Baking the Alaska
Set the oven at its maximum heat, with just one deep shelf in it. Now it is vital you *don't* bake the Alaska until the last possible moment. Plates and sauce must be ready and your guests literally waiting while it cooks. Take the Alaska from the freezer and place in the oven for 4 minutes. The meringue will scorch to a golden brown. Serve immediately, accompanied by the cassis sauce.

I cannot describe what will happen if you leave the ice-cream in the oven too long but I suggest you go back to the Italian restaurant for a slice of humble pie.

Brunch or Lunch?

There is something rather decadent about inviting people to a Sunday brunch. It implies you were at some other party until 4AM, you never have breakfast before mid-day anyway and your party is likely to begin with a Bloody Mary all round. In fact, brunch is just a convenient way of merging breakfast into lunch and not having to produce both. There are all sorts of different styles of food to serve, ranging from traditional breakfast dishes like kedgeree, to European snack dishes made from ham or cheese. Gallons of good quality coffee are essential and even if a Bloody Mary is a little over-the-top, a glass of Buck's Fizz will slip down very well.

SMOKED HADDOCK KEDGEREE
WITH TOMATO AND APPLE SALAD
SCRAMBLED EGGS WITH SMOKED SALMON
ITALIAN CIABATTA SAVOURIES
STUFFED CROISSANTS
COMPOTE OF FRUITS OF THE FOREST
TOAST AND MARMALADE

SMOKED HADDOCK KEDGEREE WITH TOMATO AND APPLE VINAIGRETTE

Kedgeree is an idea! brunch dish – it can be kept hot without deteriorating and, served with tomato and apple vinaigrette, is the perfect bridge between breakfast and lunch.

🕐 25 minutes, plus 20 minutes in the oven
Serves 8–10

450g / 1lb smoked haddock fillets
parsley sprigs, bay-leaf and peppercorns
600ml / 1 pint milk
50g / 2oz butter
175g / 6oz long-grain rice, cooked
2 hard-boiled eggs, coarsely chopped
2 tbsp chopped parsley
freshly ground black pepper
tomato and apple vinaigrette (see below)

Set the oven at 200°C/400°F/gas 6.

Place the haddock fillets in a deep baking tin with some parsley sprigs, a bay-leaf and some peppercorns. Pour the milk over and cook in the oven for 20 minutes.

Remove the fish from the tin and break it into flakes, discarding any bones or skin. Pass the cooking liquid through a sieve and keep it to one side.

Melt the butter in a clean pan and stir in the flaked fish, rice, egg and chopped parsley. Moisten the mixture with some of the fish cooking liquid and season with pepper. Either continue to heat the mixture through until hot or transfer it to an ovenproof dish and re-heat in the oven when needed.

Tomato and Apple Salad
🕐 5–10 minutes
Serves 8

4 beef tomatoes, thinly sliced
1 green apple, chopped
2 tbsp vinaigrette dressing (page 46)

Arrange the sliced tomatoes on a flat plate, scatter the apple on top and dress with the vinaigrette.

SCRAMBLED EGGS WITH SMOKED SALMON

I have had my scrambled eggs rudely described as a smashed omelette but I am unrepentant and much prefer rapidly cooked, runny scrambled eggs to the over-whisked, rubbery variety.

🕐 10 minutes
Serves 6

9 eggs
150ml / ¼ pint milk
3 tbsp double cream
salt and freshly ground black pepper
25g / 1oz butter
175g / 6oz smoked salmon pieces, cut into
   strips

Whisk the eggs together with the milk, cream and seasoning. Melt the butter in a frying pan and, once it is very hot, pour in the egg mixture. Sprinkle the smoked salmon over the eggs and whisk vigorously for a few moments, then allow the mixture to settle and cook. When the egg is beginning to set, whisk once more and immediately remove from the heat and serve.

ITALIAN CIABATTA SAVOURIES

Ciabatta is a doughy Italian bread now sold in many major stores – if you cannot find it, French bread can be substituted to make these unusual savouries. I have suggested three alternative toppings.

🕑 15 minutes, plus 10 minutes in the oven
Makes 12

12 slices ciabatta bread

Dolcelatte and Fig
(tops 12 slices)
2 tbsp olive oil
2 tbsp clear honey
225g / 8oz dolcelatte cheese, sliced
3 fresh figs, sliced

Set the oven at 200°C/400°F/gas 6.

Spread the bread with olive oil and honey. Place a layer of dolcelatte and two slices of fig on each. Bake for 10 minutes.

Avocado, Tomato and Mozzarella
(tops 12 slices)
3 tbsp olive oil
2 garlic cloves, crushed
1 avocado, peeled and sliced
4 tomatoes, sliced
175g / 6oz mozzarella cheese, sliced

Set the oven at 200°C/400°F/gas 6.

Spread a mixture of olive oil and garlic on each slice of bread. Layer alternate slices of avocado, tomato and mozzarella across the top. Bake for 10 minutes.

Smoked Ham, Beetroot and Basil
(tops 12 slices)
1 tbsp pesto sauce
12 thin slices smoked ham
3 baby beetroot, sliced
fresh basil leaves, shredded

Set the oven at 200°C/400°F/gas 6.

Spread the bread with the pesto sauce. Place a slice of ham and two slices of beetroot on each. Bake for 10 minutes and sprinkle with shredded basil after cooking.

STUFFED CROISSANTS

These 'moreish' stuffed croissants are incredibly easy to do and will be as suitable for a lunch or evening party as brunch.

🕑 15 minutes, plus 10 minutes in the oven.
Makes 12

12 small croissants, bought in

Cheese and Ham Filling
(fills 12 croissants)
75ml / 3 fl oz thick crème fraîche
a little German or English mustard
6 slices of ham
225g / 8oz Gruyère cheese, grated

Set the oven at 180°C/350°F/gas 4.

Cut a slot across each croissant without slicing it all the way through. Spread the inside with crème fraîche and a little mustard, then fill with half a slice of ham and grated cheese. Bake for 10 minutes and serve warm.

Egg and Mushroom Filling

(fills 12 croissants)
25g / 1oz margarine
225g / 8oz mushrooms, chopped
25g / 1oz plain flour
300ml / ½ pint milk
salt and freshly ground black pepper
2 hard-boiled eggs, sliced

Set the oven at 180°C/350°F/gas 4.

Again, slit open the croissants ready to fill. Melt the margarine in a pan and fry the mushrooms until tender. Sprinkle the flour on to the mushrooms and cook for a further minute. Stir in the milk, season and bring to the boil. Add the eggs and spoon the mixture into the croissants. Bake for 10 minutes and serve warm.

COMPOTE OF FRUITS OF THE FOREST

This is exactly what I would like to eat on an autumnal Sunday morning.

🕐 20 minutes, including cooking, plus 2 hours for chilling
Serves 8–10

225g / 8oz blackberries
225g / 8oz Victoria plums, stoned and sliced
2 dessert pears, peeled and sliced
2–3 tbsp caster sugar
175g / 6oz autumn raspberries or blueberries
175g / 6oz strawberries, cut into quarters
grated orange zest

Put the blackberries, plums and pears in a saucepan with 2 tablespoons of the caster sugar and heat gently. Cook the mixture for

5–10 minutes until the juice is running and the fruits have softened. Remove from the heat, stir in the raspberries and strawberries and then taste for sweetness. Add more sugar if needed. Transfer the compote to a serving dish and sprinkle grated orange zest on top. Chill before serving.

TOAST AND MARMALADE

And why not? You don't often see it in recipe books but, against all the fancy Continental pastries, croissants and brioches – 'Many people nowadays like marmalade instead.' (A.A. Milne)

fresh white and wholemeal bread
unsalted butter and good-quality, chunky marmalade

Black Treacle Tart

Crab Soufflé

Fish and Chips; Chocolate Truffle Cake with Prunes and Armagnac

Swiss Cheese Fondue with Cured Meats and Accompaniments

Growing Old Gracefully

Who among your friends do you know well enough to tell you have invited them to a dinner party entitled 'growing old gracefully'? Oh, it will be a lovely occasion – gentlemen in jackets and ties, place-cards on the table, wine in decanters, a quite sublime menu and everyone home and in bed by 11.30PM, but will you admit to it?

CRAB SOUFFLES

....

ROAST PARTRIDGE
WITH DAMSON AND WILD RICE STUFFING
GAME CHIPS
PARSNIP PUREE
RUNNER BEANS

....

PEARS POACHED IN BEAUMES-DE-VENISE

CRAB SOUFFLES

A good soufflé should be light, tasty and leave you wishing you could have just a little bit more. I think they are excellent dishes for dinner parties, especially as you can prepare them in advance. Yes, as long as your soufflés are refrigerated, you can make them up to 2 hours beforehand and then just pop them in the oven when needed.

🕐 15 minutes, plus 15 minutes in the oven
Serves 6

20g / ¾oz margarine
20g / ¾oz plain flour
150ml / ¼ pint milk
175g / 6oz canned or frozen, brown or white crab meat
4 egg yolks
salt and freshly ground black pepper
½ tsp Tabasco
2 tsp Dijon mustard
1 tbsp grated Parmesan cheese
6 egg whites

Preparation
Melt the margarine in a pan and stir in the flour. Cook for 1 minute, then stir in the milk. Continue stirring until smooth. Remove from the heat and add the crab meat, followed by the egg yolks. Season well with salt and pepper, and add the Tabasco, Dijon mustard and Parmesan cheese. Whisk the egg whites in a separate bowl until very stiff. Using a metal spoon, fold the whites into the mixture.

Here lies the secret of soufflé making – the more you 'fold', the more you flatten the whites, making the soufflé heavier. I recommend you fold half the whites in to begin with; when this is well mixed, add the other half and hardly fold this in at all.

Spoon the mixture into individual ramekins and refrigerate until ready to cook.

Cooking
Set the oven at 180°C/350°F/gas 4.

Cook the soufflés for 15 minutes and serve immediately.

ROAST PARTRIDGE WITH DAMSON AND WILD RICE STUFFING

Although partridge costs the earth, it is wonderful to eat and worth splashing out once in a while. Alternatively, you can make this dish using poussin. I recommend serving some game chips, parsnip purée and runner beans (or your favourite green vegetable) with it.

🕐 45 minutes, plus 45 minutes in the oven
Serves 6

6 dressed partridges
extra cooked damsons and flat-leafed parsley to decorate

Stuffing
100 g / 4oz damsons, cooked, stoned and sweetened with brown sugar
50g / 2oz wild rice, cooked
75g / 3oz cream cheese
25g / 1oz soft breadcrumbs
1 tbsp clear honey
salt and freshly ground black pepper

Sauce
300ml / ½ pint white wine
300ml / ½ pint chicken stock
cayenne pepper
salt
3 tbsp mayonnaise (page 62)

Preparation

The partridges can be stuffed and ready to cook but should only go into the oven an hour before eating. The sauce will make itself as the birds cook.

Blend all the ingredients for the stuffing together until the damsons have broken up slightly. Using a piping bag or small spoon, fill the cavity of each bird with the stuffing.

Arrange the birds upside-down in a deep roasting tin and pour the white wine and stock over them.

Cooking and serving

Set the oven at 200°C/400°F/gas 6.

Cook the partridges in the bottom of the oven for 30 minutes. Then turn the birds breast-side up and cook for a further 15 minutes.

Transfer the partridges to a serving dish and keep warm. Place the roasting tin directly on the hob and bring the cooking liquid to a rapid boil. Season with salt and cayenne pepper. Remove from the heat and whisk in the mayonnaise. Transfer to a bowl and keep warm.

Decorate the partridges with sprigs of flat-leafed parsley and an extra spoonful of damsons.

PEARS POACHED IN BEAUMES-DE-VENISE

A delicious, light fruit dessert that can be enhanced by serving a small glass of the remaining Beaumes-de-Venise with it.

🕐 45 minutes, including cooking
Serves 6

6 firm Conference pears
300ml / ½ pint Beaumes-de-Venise
300ml / ½ pint cold water
50g / 2oz caster sugar
1 cinnamon stick
grated zest of ½ lemon
grated zest of ½ orange
1 tbsp cornflour
lemon balm to decorate

Peel the pears, leaving the stalks on, and then, using a corer, cut the core out through a hole in the base.

Put the Beaumes-de-Venise, water, sugar, cinnamon, lemon and orange zest in a saucepan over a gentle heat. Add the pears and place a plate on top to weight them down into the liquid. Cover the pan and simmer for 20 minutes.

Lift the pears out of the liquid and arrange them in a serving dish. Spoon a little of the cooking liquid into a cup and mix it with cornflour. Pour this back into the pan, mix well and bring to the boil. Cook for 1 minute, then pour over the pears and leave to cool completely.

Decorate the pears with leaves of lemon balm and, if you like, serve with lightly whipped cream.

Witches and Bonfires

American-style Hallowe'en and the tradition of Guy Fawkes combine rather well in Britain. After everyone has done their duty standing outside around the bonfire with trickles of rain seeping inside their collars, a wholesome seasonal supper is just what's needed.

SMOKED CHICKEN AND CELERY SOUP

CARBONADE OF BEEF WITH MUSTARD CROUTES
JACKET POTATOES WITH FROMAGE FRAIS AND CHIVES
DEVILLED PUMPKIN
VEGETABLE MEDLEY

BLACK TREACLE TART

SMOKED CHICKEN AND CELERY SOUP

In case you are not smoked enough from the bonfire, a bowlful of this will ensure the warm smoky flavour is right on the inside.

🕐 40 minutes, including cooking
Serves 6–8

15g / ½oz margarine
½ bunch celery, chopped
225g / 8oz potatoes, diced
600ml / 1 pint chicken stock
600ml / 1 pint milk
225g / 8oz smoked chicken, finely chopped
1 tbsp chopped parsley
a few drops of Tabasco
salt and freshly ground black pepper

Melt the margarine in a large saucepan and toss the celery and potato in it for 2 minutes. Add the stock and bring to the boil. Simmer for 20 minutes, then transfer the mixture to a food processor and reduce to a purée.

Return the mixture to the saucepan, add the milk, smoked chicken, chopped parsley and season well with Tabasco, salt and pepper. Bring the soup to the boil just before serving.

🌰

CARBONADE OF BEEF WITH MUSTARD CROUTES

Beef cooked slowly in stout and topped with mustard croûtes is perfect for a cold autumn night. It has a mellow oaky flavour rather akin to Rioja wine – in fact that's what I think we should drink with it.

🕐 20 minutes, plus 1½–2 hours in the oven
Serves 6–8

50g / 2oz margarine
2 large onions, chopped
900g / 2lb good, lean stewing steak, fully trimmed and diced
50g / 2oz plain flour
salt and freshly ground black pepper
600ml / 1 pint stout
300ml / ½ pint beef stock
2 tbsp dark brown sugar
2 tbsp red wine vinegar
450g / 1lb button mushrooms

Mustard Croûtes
½ stick French bread
French mustard

Preparation
Heat the margarine in a large saucepan and fry the onions until lightly browned. Roll the prepared meat in the flour and season well with salt and pepper. Add the beef and flour to the onion and fry for a further 5 minutes. Once the meat is browned all over, pour in the stout and stock. Add the sugar, vinegar and mushrooms. Cook over a low heat for 1½ hours, stirring occasionally. Once the meat is tender, the carbonade can be left to cool and then re-heated when needed.

Cut the French bread into 1-cm/½-inch thick slices and spread these with French mustard.

Re-heating and serving
The carbonade can either be transferred to a casserole and placed in a moderate oven (180°C/350°F/gas 4) for 30 minutes with the bread croûtes around the top, or it can be re-heated in a saucepan on the hob, and the croûtes popped into the oven to heat through.

JACKET POTATOES WITH FROMAGE FRAIS AND CHIVES

I am not really going to lecture you on how to cook a jacket potato, but they are traditional with bonfires and I include them as the best possible accompaniment to the carbonade (page 93).

🕐 Could be hours!
Serves 6

12 (175g / 6oz) potatoes
rock salt

Filling
175ml / 6 fl oz fromage frais
1 tbsp snipped fresh chives
salt and freshly ground black pepper

The charcoal effect: salt and wrap six potatoes in a double layer of foil. Using a spade, scrape some very hot ashes away from the centre of the bonfire and bury the potatoes in them. Leave them for 1 hour and hope for the best. They will either be raw or blackened or perfect! Bake the other six in the oven to hedge your bets.

Mix the fromage frais with the chives, salt and pepper and serve in a separate dish to dollop on to the potatoes.

DEVILLED PUMPKIN

The perfect use for the flesh of the pumpkin lantern your children have insisted on making.

🕐 1 hour, including cooking
Serves 6–8

675g / 1½lb pumpkin flesh, diced
25g / 1oz butter
2 tsp Worcestershire sauce
1 tsp ground ginger
1 tsp ground cinnamon
a few drops of Tabasco
2 tbsp double cream
1 tbsp maple syrup
salt and freshly ground black pepper

Cook the diced pumpkin in boiling salted water for 40 minutes. Drain, then return the vegetable to the pan and stir in all the other ingredients. Allow to simmer for 10 minutes.

Transfer the devilled pumpkin to an ovenproof serving dish and either keep warm in a low oven or re-heat when required.

VEGETABLE MEDLEY

This menu seems to be a spectrum of autumnal browns and oranges. I suggest a mixture of bright green vegetables should be added to revive it.

🕐 15 minutes, including cooking
Serves 6–8

175g / 6oz French beans, topped, tailed and
*   halved*
175g / 6oz courgettes, sliced
175g / 6oz mangetout, stalks removed
25g / 1oz margarine

Bring a large pan of salted water to the boil. Plunge the French beans into it and cook for about 5 minutes until the beans are soft. Add the courgettes, allow 1 minute for the water to reboil, then add the mangetout and drain. Refresh the vegetables briefly under the cold tap without allowing them to chill.

Transfer the vegetables to a serving dish and dot with knobs of margarine. If dinner is not imminent, allow the dish to cool and re-heat in the oven when required.

BLACK TREACLE TART

A real Hallowe'en pud: the wing of a bat, the eye of a toad and black treacle tart dotted with glowing, red cherry embers.

🕐 30 minutes, plus 15 minutes for maturing and 25 minutes in the oven
Serves 6–8

Rich Shortcrust Pastry
175g / 6oz plain flour
¼ tsp salt
100g / 4oz butter, cut in knobs
2 egg yolks
2 tbsp cold water

Filling
225g / 8oz black treacle
225g / 8oz golden syrup
grated rind and juice of 1 lemon
⅓ loaf stale white bread, made into
*   breadcrumbs*
75g / 3oz glacé cherries

Set the oven at 200°/400°F/gas 6. Oil a 20-cm/8-inch flan tin.

Put the flour and salt in a bowl and rub in the butter. Mix the yolks and water, pour this into a well in the flour and knead the

pastry firmly. Roll the pastry out on a floured surface and carefully fit it into the tin, pinching off any excess around the edges. Prick the base all over with a fork, then bake 'blind' (page 00) for 10 minutes and open for a further 10 minutes.

To make the filling, heat the treacle, syrup and lemon rind and juice in a saucepan. Remove from the heat, stir in the breadcrumbs and leave for 15 minutes to mature! Pour the mixture into the flan case and dot glacé cherries over the top of it. Bake for 25 minutes.

Either keep warm or re-heat when needed.

ENTERTAINING IN THE
Winter

We need to look at winter in two stages; the chaos of Christmas and the void that lies beyond.

Christmas itself is the most prolific season for entertaining. There are office parties, family parties, friends' parties and, yes, this year you will have to invite the neighbours in. Food can be a wonderful mixture of traditional and creative festive fare and I have given some examples of combining the two.

Then, after Christmas, comes that 'gloom-and-doom' time of year – you can't afford to go skiing, it seems to be dark more or less continuously and there is nothing to be cheerful about, so why on earth should you be cheerful? This is surely when you should throw yourself into entertaining. Have a fondue evening, celebrate Chinese New Year or simply invite friends round for an informal supper – cheer up!

Christmas Bash —
A Drinks Party for 20

There was a time when all you needed for a good Christmas drinks do was a couple of Party-7s and a box of mince pies. (For the benefit of the younger readers, a Party-7 was a seven-pint tin of rather watery beer – I won't tell you what the mince pies were like.) Alas, nowadays we are all much more sophisticated and Christmas parties compete with one another for position in the league. I wouldn't bother – just give them 'fish and chips'.

FISH AND CHIPS
CHIPOLATAS AND CHESTNUTS
STUFFED FRESH DATES
TURKEY AND CRANBERRY CRACKERS
SAVOURY TARTLETS
SMOKED SALMON DIP WITH CRUDITES
AND BREAD STICKS
CANDIED PEEL

FISH AND CHIPS

It takes a great deal of style to invite your poshest friends over for drinks and then just serve up fish and chips. This recipe has all the style needed to get away with it.

We are going to make tiny pieces of fish and chips, served in miniature 'paper' cones which can all be eaten in a single mouthful.

🕐 40 minutes, including cooking
Makes 30 items

450g / 1lb plaice fillets
2 eggs
dry breadcrumbs
350g / 12oz potatoes, peeled
oil for frying
distilled vinegar
salt
225g / 8oz filo pastry

Preparation
Cut the fish into small strips about 4cm/1½ inches long and 1cm/½ inch wide. Whisk the eggs with a little salt. Dip the fish pieces in the egg, then roll them in breadcrumbs. Cut the potatoes into tiny chips 5cm/2 inches long and 3mm/⅛ inch wide. Heat a pan of deep oil and first fry the chips, then the fish until cooked. Sprinkle with salt and vinegar while still hot.

Lay the filo pastry out on your work surface and cut into even rectangles 10 × 5cm/4 × 2 inches. Use two sheets of pastry (double thickness) and fold them into a cone shape. Place a piece of fish and two or three chips inside and lay the cones on an oiled baking tin. They can now be left until you are ready to serve them.

Final cooking and serving
Set the oven at 200°C/400°F/gas 6.

Bake the fish and chips in small batches for just 5 minutes and serve immediately.

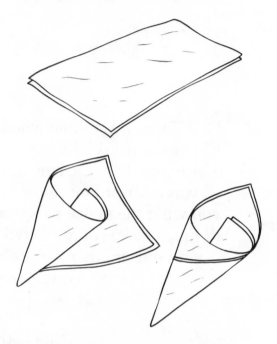

Fold double thicknesses of filo pastry into cones.

CHIPOLATAS AND CHESTNUTS

Buy the miniature cocktail-size sausages and, let me warn you, buy lots – they will all be eaten.

🕐 30 minutes, plus 25 minutes in the oven
Makes 32

32 cocktail sausages, separated and pricked
50g / 2oz lard
2 tbsp clear honey
1 tsp dried or fresh rosemary
½ tsp French mustard
450g / 1lb fresh chestnuts, baked and shelled

Set oven at 200°C/400°F/gas 6.

Melt the lard in a roasting tin and roast the sausages in it for 15 minutes. Melt the honey in a little pan with the rosemary and mustard. Take the sausages out of the oven and drain off most of the fat. Pour the honey mixture over and roll the sausages in it. Return them to the oven for a further 10 minutes.

Skewer a half-chestnut and a sausage on to individual wooden cocktail sticks. Re-heat in the oven just before serving.

STUFFED FRESH DATES

These spicy dates are both sticky and 'moreish'. The same method can be used to stuff prunes and you could alternate the two on a dish.

🕒 20 minutes, plus 2 hours for chilling
Makes 20

20 fresh dates
100g / 4oz cream cheese
½ tsp ground cinnamon
½ tsp mixed spice
1 tsp lemon juice
75g / 3oz peanuts, chopped

Slit the dates open lengthways and remove the stones. Mix the cream cheese with the cinnamon, mixed spice and lemon juice. Pipe this mixture into each date. Dip the dates, cheese-side down, into the chopped peanuts and leave to chill before serving.

TURKEY AND CRANBERRY CRACKERS

A glorified sausage roll but made with leftover turkey and cranberry sauce.

🕒 30 minutes, plus 15 minutes in the oven
Makes 20 crackers

450g / 1lb frozen puff pastry, thawed
350g / 12oz cooked turkey meat, finely
*   chopped*
2 tbsp cranberry sauce or jelly
salt and freshly ground black pepper
egg wash (whole egg mixed with salt)

Set the oven at 200°C/400°F/gas 6. Oil a baking sheet.

Roll out the pastry to a thickness of 3mm/ ⅛ inch. Cut into 10-cm/4-inch squares.

Mix the turkey meat with the cranberry sauce or jelly and season well. Place a dessertspoonful of this mixture in the centre of each square and roll the pastry into a cylinder. Brush the join with water to secure the edges. Twist each end of the pastry in towards the filling, to form a cracker. Brush the crackers with egg wash and bake for 15 minutes.

The turkey crackers can be re-heated or served cold.

SAVOURY TARTLETS

Miniature meals served in individual tartlet cases for finger eating. Once you have made the pastry cases, there is no limit to the range of different leftovers you can revamp as fillings.

🕐 25–30 minutes, depending on chosen filling, plus 15 minutes in the oven

Pastry Cases
350g / 12oz shortcrust pastry for 12 tartlets

Set the oven at 200°C/400°F/gas 6. Oil a 7.5-cm/3-inch tartlet sheet.

Roll out the pastry to a thickness of 3mm/⅛ inch. Cut it into rounds with a 9-cm/3½-inch pastry cutter. Fit the rounds into the tartlet sheet and prick the base of each pastry case with a fork.

Now, the pastry needs to be baked blind and you will need to fit each round with a tiny piece of greaseproof paper and some baking rice. Alternatively, you can invest in a second tartlet sheet and simply sit this on top of the pastry to hold it down.

Bake blind for 10 minutes, then remove the greaseproof paper and rice (or top tin) and cook for a further 5 minutes.

Stilton and Apple Filling
(Fills 12 tartlets)
1 Bramley apple, cored and sliced
a little butter
salt and freshly ground black pepper
150g / 5oz Stilton cheese, sliced
parsley sprig

Fry the apple in a little melted butter until soft. Season with salt and pepper. Spoon the apple into the pastry cases. Add a slice of Stilton and return the tartlets to the oven (still set at 200°C/400°F/gas 6) for 5 minutes to melt the cheese. Add a sprig of parsley and serve hot or cold.

Smoked Mackerel and Horseradish
(Fills 12 tartlets)
2 smoked mackerel fillets
6 tsp horseradish sauce
a little leftover salad
freshly ground black pepper

Skin the mackerel fillets and flake the flesh. Dollop half a teaspoon of horseradish sauce into each pastry case and arrange the mackerel and a little finely chopped salad on top. Grind black pepper over.

Ham with Spiced Tangerine
(Fills 12 tartlets)
3 tangerines
2 tsp white wine vinegar
grated nutmeg
salt and freshly ground black pepper
2 tbsp mayonnaise (page 62)
175g / 6oz thinly sliced ham

Peel and segment the tangerines and mix with the vinegar, nutmeg and seasoning in a bowl. Leave for 1 hour to marinate. Spoon a little mayonnaise into each tartlet case, place a folded piece of ham on top and a couple of segments of tangerine on top of that.

SMOKED SALMON DIP WITH CRUDITES AND BREAD STICKS

Just something to leave on the side; you will be surprised how quickly it disappears.

🕐 15 minutes
Serves 20

225g / 8oz smoked salmon pieces
175g / 6oz cream cheese
1 tbsp lemon juice
2 tsp chopped fresh dill
salt and freshly ground black pepper
150ml / ¼ pint soured cream

Crudités
1 bunch radishes
1 cucumber, cut into sticks
2 yellow peppers, cut into strips
2 packets bread sticks
fresh dill sprig to decorate

In a food processor, chop the smoked salmon into very small pieces, then add all the other dip ingredients and seasoning. Once the mixture is fully blended, transfer it to a small serving bowl. Decorate the top with a sprig of dill and arrange breadsticks and crudités alongside.

CANDIED PEEL

Somehow this is very Christmassy and you will be proud to tell your friends you made it yourself.

🕐 40 minutes, plus 3 hours for cooling and drying
Makes 40–50 pieces

1 orange
1 lemon
1 lime
100g / 4oz caster sugar
50g / 2oz granulated sugar

Cut the fruit into quarters and then scoop off the flesh. Cut the sections of peel into long strips and press the flesh through a sieve to extract the juice.

Bring a saucepan of water to the boil and cook the strips of peel in it for 10 minutes; drain.

In a separate pan, heat the sugar and fruit juices together gently until the sugar has dissolved. Add the peel and simmer for 10 minutes. Remove from the heat and allow the syrup to cool for 2 hours with the strips of peel in it.

Scoop out the citrus strips with a slotted spoon and place them on a wire rack to dry. Leave for an hour and then roll them in granulated sugar.

Pre-ski, Apres-ski or No-ski at All

Whichever category you belong to, I can think of nothing nicer than sitting by a fire with friends on a cold winter evening, eating a delicious fondue and reminiscing about that black run you never quite went down.

MUSHROOM AND CORIANDER SOUP

....

SWISS CHEESE FONDUE WITH CURED MEATS AND ACCOMPANIMENTS

....

CHOCOLATE TRUFFLE CAKE WITH PRUNES AND ARMAGNAC

MUSHROOM AND CORIANDER SOUP

This unusual soup has a mild oriental flavour to tantalize the taste-buds at the start of the meal. A glass of dry sherry would be an excellent accompaniment.

🕐 45 minutes, including cooking
Serves 6

450g / 1lb mushrooms
2 tsp coriander seeds
small bunch fresh coriander
900ml / 1½ pints chicken stock (2 stock
  cubes dissolved in water will do)
salt and freshly ground black pepper
50g / 2oz margarine
50g / 2oz plain flour
300ml / ½ pint single cream

Purée the mushrooms and coriander seeds and some of the fresh coriander in a food processor. Save the remaining coriander leaves to decorate.

Transfer the mixture to a large saucepan. Add the chicken stock, bring to the boil and cook for 15 minutes. Now, if you have such a thing, pass the mixture through a mouli-grinder to remove the husks of the coriander seeds (if you don't have one, just decide to have your soup crunchy!).

Return the liquid to the pan, bring back to the boil and season well. Mix the margarine and flour together and drop small pieces into the soup. Whisk the soup until all the margarine and flour has disappeared and the soup has thickened. Remove from the heat and stir in the single cream.

The soup can be re-heated when needed and served decorated with coriander leaves.

❧

SWISS CHEESE FONDUE WITH CURED MEATS AND ACCOMPANIMENTS

This is the first recipe I ever learned as a lower-than-low apprentice in Switzerland twenty years ago and it is still one of my favourites. The secrets of a good fondue are minimum flour and the use of a delicate white wine.

🕐 15–20 minutes, including cooking
Serves 6

225g / 8oz Gruyère cheese, grated
225g / 8oz Emmental cheese, grated
2 tbsp plain flour
freshly grated nutmeg
salt and freshly ground black pepper
600ml / 1 pint white wine
2 garlic cloves, crushed
kirsch

Accompaniments
yards of crispy French bread, diced
selection of cured meats
pickled onions
small gherkins

Mix the two cheeses with the flour, nutmeg, a little salt and lots of black pepper. Work these dry ingredients together with your hands. Heat the white wine and garlic in a fondue pot and bring to the boil. Whisk in the cheese mixture and cook until the fondue is thick and smooth. Add a good slug of kirsch, grind extra black pepper on top and serve on a fondue burner placed in the centre of the table.

As well as French bread I like to serve a selection of thinly sliced cured meats and bowls of onions and gherkins. These can all be dipped in the fondue or just eaten with it.

❧

CHOCOLATE TRUFFLE CAKE WITH PRUNES AND ARMAGNAC

This truly indulgent pudding would make an excellent substitute birthday cake with the odd candle stuck in the top.

🕐 30 minutes, plus at least 12 hours for soaking
Serves 6

12 prunes, stoned and halved
50ml / 2 fl oz Armagnac
8 digestive biscuits
50g / 2oz butter, melted
100ml / 4 fl oz cold water
575g / 1¼lb bitter or plain chocolate
75g / 3oz butter
300ml / ½ pint double cream
cocoa powder to dust
fresh fruit or flowers to decorate

Soak the prunes in the Armagnac well in advance. Do a few extra in case you indulge in sampling while you are preparing this dish.

Crumble the digestive biscuits and mix with the melted butter. Press this mixture evenly across the base of a loose-bottomed 20-cm/8-inch cake tin.

Put the water and chocolate in a pan and melt the chocolate over a very gentle heat, stirring occasionally. Once smooth, remove from the heat and whisk in small knobs of the butter. Continue to beat until the butter has completely disappeared. Whip the double cream in a separate bowl and fold this into the chocolate. Add the prunes and pour the mixture into the flan tin. Leave to set overnight.

Ease the truffle cake gently out of the tin – you may need to use a hot knife around the edge. Transfer to a serving plate and dust the top with cocoa powder. Decorate with fresh fruit or flowers.

Christmas Day in the kitchen
Red Mullet with Beanshoots and Coriander
Chicken Liver and Croûton Salad
Baked Oysters and Artichokes in Champagne Sauce

Taking on Christmas Dinner and Surviving

How often have you said to yourself that Christmas would
be fine if you did not have to feed everyone, or the Yuletide
feast would be easy if you did not have to produce it at
Christmas? If I told you, however, to cook the whole thing
days beforehand, let your turkey get cold, then carve it
with the greatest of ease, prepare all the sauces and
vegetables and gently reheat them on Christmas Day – you
would accuse me of cheating. And besides, it would not be
Christmas without crisis point at noon, tears at one and
champagne with smiles some time later.

PINK GRAPEFRUIT WITH PORT

....

ROAST TURKEY WITH CHESTNUT STUFFING
GRAVY, BREAD SAUCE AND CRANBERRY SAUCE
CHIPOLATA SAUSAGES AND BACON ROLLS
ROAST POTATOES AND PARSNIPS
CARROTS AND BRUSSELS SPROUTS

....

PLUM PUDDING
BRANDY BUTTER

PINK GRAPEFRUIT WITH PORT

A starter may seem unnecessary with so much to eat afterwards but it will serve the purpose of beginning the meal with relative order before the main course is served. A simple appetizer of pink grapefruit with port is ideal.

🕐 10 minutes, plus 2 hours for chilling
Serves 6

3 pink grapefruit
6 tbsp ruby port

Halve the grapefruit and then take care to cut each segment free of the pith individually. Spoon the port over the grapefruit and chill before serving.

ROAST TURKEY WITH CHESTNUT STUFFING

I am a great believer in roasting the turkey quickly and at a high temperature but cooking times will vary according to the size of the bird.

🕐 About 45 minutes for the stuffing, plus variable times in the oven and 30 minutes for resting turkey!

3.5-kg / 8-lb turkey (serves 6–10) – 1½
hours wrapped and 10 minutes open
5.5-kg / 12-lb turkey (serves 10–16) – 2
hours wrapped and 15 minutes open
7-kg / 16-lb turkey (serves 16–20) – 2½
hours wrapped and 20 minutes open

Stuffing
(for a 5.5-kg / 12-lb turkey)
450g / 1lb chestnuts (canned or fresh and
peeled), chopped
225g / 8oz breadcrumbs
75g / 3oz soft breadcrumbs
salt and freshly ground black pepper
chopped parsley

Christmas Eve
Blend all the ingredients for the stuffing together and fill the turkey's front end (between the breasts) with the mixture. Wrap the skin tightly over the stuffing and secure it underneath with two wooden cocktail sticks; the larger cavity can also be stuffed if required. Lay out two large sheets of foil, brush these with oil and wrap the turkey into a sealed parcel. Transfer to a roasting tin ready to cook the next day.

Christmas Day
Set the oven at 220°C/425°F/gas 7.

Cook the turkey for the time suggested above, then remove the foil, drain the fat into a saucepan to make gravy and return the bird to the oven to brown. Once fully cooked, rest the turkey for at least 30 minutes before carving. To keep it warm, re-wrap in foil and cover with layer upon layer of tea-towels.

Gravy, Bread Sauce and Cranberry Sauce
The gravy will have to be made after the turkey is cooked but the bread sauce and cranberry sauce are other jobs that can be done on Christmas Eve.

🕐 About 1 hour, depending on number of interruptions, plus 1 hour for infusing!

Gravy
Makes about 900ml / 1½ pints

turkey dripping
50g / 2oz plain flour
125ml / 4fl oz white wine
600ml / 1 pint cold water
½ chicken stock cube
2 tbsp apricot jam
1 tbsp lemon juice
salt and freshly ground black pepper

Melt the dripping in a pan, stir in the flour and cook for 2 minutes. Add the white wine and water, stirring continuously, and bring to the boil. Crumble in the stock cube and add the jam, lemon juice, salt and pepper.

Bread Sauce
Makes about 600ml / 1 pint

600ml / 1 pint milk
1 onion, chopped
1 tsp whole cloves
1 tsp mace
100g / 4oz breadcrumbs
50g / 2oz butter

Heat the milk, onion, cloves and mace in a saucepan and bring to the boil. Remove from the heat and leave to infuse for 1 hour. Strain the milk, return it to the pan, stir in the breadcrumbs and butter and bring back to the boil. Serve warm.

Cranberry Sauce
Makes about 600ml / 1 pint

450g / 1lb fresh cranberries
grated zest and juice of 1 orange
300ml / ½ pint cold water
175g / 6oz caster sugar

Put the ingredients in a pan and cook until the cranberries pop open. Serve warm or cold.

Chipolata Sausages and Bacon Rolls
Serves 6–8

12 chipolatas
12 bacon rashers, rinds removed, (rolled and skewered on wooden cocktail sticks)

Cook these in the oven at 180°C/350°F/gas 4 for 20 minutes on Christmas Eve and simply re-heat before the meal is served.

Roast Potatoes and Parsnips
🕐 20 minutes, plus about 1½ hours in the oven
Serves 6–8

100g / 4oz lard
1.5kg / 3lb old potatoes, peeled and cut into serving pieces
900g / 2lb parsnips, cut into serving pieces

Set the oven at 220°C/425°F/gas 7.

Melt the lard in a separate roasting tin. Make sure the potatoes are dry and roll them in the lard before placing the tin in the top of the oven. Turn the potatoes after 15 minutes, then return to the oven for 30 minutes. Turn the potatoes again, add the parsnips and roast together until golden-brown.

Carrots and Brussels Sprouts
🕐 About 40 minutes, including cooking
Serves 6–8

675g / 1½lb carrots, sliced
675g / 1½lb sprouts, prepared
25g / 1oz butter

Cook these vegetables in separate pans well before the meal is to be served. When tender but still firm, drain and refresh under cold water. Place a knob of butter in the bottom of a pan and the vegetables on top. Re-heat, covered, over a low heat just before serving.

PLUM PUDDING

This must, of course, be made well in advance and steamed on Christmas Day. There are lots of good ready-made puddings on the market but, as this is one element of Christmas which can be dealt with on a dull day in November, you might like the satisfaction of making your own.

🕐 20 minutes, plus 4 hours and 2 hours for boiling
Serves 6–8

Dry ingredients
100g / 4oz suet
100g / 4oz self-raising flour
75g / 3oz soft breadcrumbs
75g / 3oz soft brown sugar
50g / 2oz ground almonds
225g / 8oz raisins
225g / 8oz sultanas
75g / 3oz dried apricots, diced
75g / 3oz glacé cherries, diced
2 tsp ground mixed spice
½ tsp salt

Wet ingredients
3 eggs
2 tbsp black treacle
150ml / ¼ pint stout
grated zest of 2 oranges

To 'feed' the pudding
4 tbsp brandy

Mix all the dry ingredients together, then blend in the wet ingredients and make a huge wish for something wonderful. Transfer the mixture to a buttered 1.75-litre/3-pint china pudding basin, place a piece of buttered greaseproof paper on top and tie a piece of cloth over it.

Sit the pudding in a saucepan of water filled to just below the top of the basin. Boil gently for 4 hours over a low heat with the lid on the pan, topping up with water every now and then; don't allow the pan to boil dry.

Store the pudding in a cool dry place. Then a week before Christmas unwrap it, spike the pudding with holes and 'feed' it with brandy.

Christmas Day
Steam the pudding in a saucepan of water (as above) for 2 hours before turning it out on to a hot dish. Decorate with holly, flame with warmed brandy and serve with brandy butter (below). Sing 'Jingle Bells' heartily!

Brandy Butter
10 minutes
Serves 6–8

225g / 8oz unsalted butter
225g / 8oz caster sugar
3 tbsp brandy

Blend the butter and sugar together and then add the brandy slowly a little at a time.

Serving Christmas dinner
I hate to imagine it, either everyone helps or no-one does – either way is hopeless. Make sure the plates and serving dishes are really hot to give you a sporting chance of a hot meal.

Chinese New Year

'The year of the Red Herring' sounds a lot less frightening than dragons or horses and a good beginning for an outrageous, fun evening. I have not included any starter dishes on this menu but a trip to a Chinese supermarket should provide you with all sorts of crispy wonton, dumplings, spring rolls, prawn crackers and so on.

The main dishes in these recipes nearly all need finishing at the last moment in quick succession: lots of chef stress, I am afraid. They should then be placed on the table together, allowing guests to struggle with chopsticks and help themselves as they please.

CANTONESE PORK WITH SQUID

SPICY LEMON CHICKEN

EGG-FRIED RICE

VEGETABLE STIR-FRY

RED MULLET WITH BEANSHOOTS AND CORIANDER

....

PINEAPPLE DELIGHT
WITH LYCHEE FLOWERS

CANTONESE PORK
WITH SQUID

I am sorry there are so many ingredients in
this recipe and, if you cannot find them all,
just sling in something else instead. As long
as it's not the Chinese Ambassador who is
coming to dinner, no one will know the
difference. (By the way, if he is coming, give
him Shepherd's Pie – I know he likes that.)

🕐 30 minutes, plus 3–6 hours for
marinating and 40 minutes in the oven
Serves 6

450g / 1lb pork tenderloin, fully trimmed
4 tbsp sunflower oil
1 garlic clove, crushed
2 tbsp fine strips of root ginger
225g / 8oz squid, prepared and cut into
    strips
1 red pepper, cut into diamonds
1 yellow pepper, cut into diamonds
1 tbsp black bean sauce (optional)
1 heaped tbsp cornflour, dissolved in a little
    cold water

Marinade
2 garlic cloves, crushed
1 tbsp grated root ginger
3 tbsp soy sauce
3 tbsp sunflower oil
1 tbsp clear honey
1 tbsp hoisin sauce
6 tbsp dry sherry
2 tsp five-spice powder

Preparation
Mix all the marinade ingredients together
and roll the pork in it. Leave to marinate for
3–6 hours.

Set the oven at 200°C/400°F/gas 6. Roast
the pork in its marinade for 40 minutes.
Allow to cool and then slice the meat into

1-cm/½-inch thick discs. Save all the
remaining juices from the roasting tin.

Prepare all the other ingredients ready for
cooking at the last moment.

Final cooking and serving
Heat the sunflower oil in a wok and add the
garlic, ginger, squid and peppers. Cook for
3–4 minutes, stirring occasionally. Now stir
in the black bean sauce, sliced pork and all
the cooking juices, plus 150ml/¼ pint of
water. Bring to the boil and stir in the
dissolved cornflour to thicken. Transfer to a
serving dish and serve immediately.

SPICY LEMON
CHICKEN

This dish can be as spicy as you like – just
increase or decrease the chilli.

🕐 25–30 minutes, including cooking
Serves 6

3 (225g / 8oz) chicken breasts, cut into
    7.5-cm/3-inch long strips
2 egg whites
1 tbsp cornflour
150ml / ¼ pint sunflower or groundnut oil
300ml / ½ pint chicken stock
grated zest and juice of 1 large lemon
6 tbsp dry sherry
1 garlic clove, crushed
1 tbsp chilli sauce
1 tbsp soy sauce
2 tsp caster sugar
1 tbsp cornflour, dissolved in a little cold
    water
1 bunch spring onions, finely chopped

Preparation

Blend the egg whites and 1 tablespoon cornflour together and roll the chicken pieces in it until well-coated. Heat the oil in a wok and fry the chicken for 2 minutes. Remove the chicken from the oil and place on kitchen paper towels; allow to cool. Assemble all the other ingredients ready for cooking.

Final cooking and serving

Heat the chicken stock, lemon, sherry, garlic, chilli sauce, soy sauce and sugar in a saucepan or wok. Bring to the boil, then stir in the dissolved cornflour to thicken the sauce. Add the chicken, cook for 1 minute until very hot and then transfer the whole lot to a serving dish. Sprinkle the spring onions over the top.

EGG-FRIED RICE

The key to getting that light, fluffy rice the Chinese are so good at is to wash it really well in a large sieve both before and after cooking. This gets rid of the surface starch which sticks the grains together.

🕐 30 minutes, including cooking
Serves 6

3 tbsp sunflower or groundnut oil
450g / 1lb long-grain rice, cooked
  beautifully
2 eggs, whisked
salt and white pepper

Heat the oil in a wok until it is very hot. Add the rice and stir-fry for a few moments, then add the seasoned eggs and continue to stir-fry until the egg is lightly cooked. Transfer to a serving dish.

VEGETABLE STIR-FRY

Practically any variety of vegetables can be used in a stir-fry as long as you blanch them individually beforehand. Choose an interesting selection of colours and shapes.

🕐 20 minutes, plus about 20 minutes for cooking
Serves 6

225g / 8oz white radish or turnip, peeled
  and diced
225g / 8oz carrots, peeled and sliced
175g / 6oz mangetout, topped and tailed
1 red pepper, diced
1 (350g / 12oz) can water chestnuts, drained
  and halved
1 (350g / 12oz) can baby corn, sliced on an
  angle
150ml / ¼ pint sunflower or groundnut oil
1 garlic clove, crushed
sesame seeds
sesame oil

Preparation

Cook the turnips and carrots in boiling water until tender but still firm. Drain and refresh them in cold or iced water. Plunge the mangetout and red pepper into boiling water, then drain almost immediately and chill.

Final cooking and serving

Heat the cooking oil in a wok until very hot. Season the oil with garlic, then add all the vegetables and fry vigorously for 2 minutes. Transfer to a serving dish and sprinkle with sesame seeds and a few drops of sesame oil. Serve as soon as possible.

RED MULLET WITH BEANSHOOTS AND CORIANDER

A stuffed fish cooked in its own juices is a delicious, easy-on-the-cook recipe. All sorts of different fish and less 'Chinesey' stuffings can be substituted using the same basic method.

🕐 15 minutes, plus 20 minutes in the oven
Serves 6

100g / 4oz beanshoots
1 tbsp fine strips of root ginger
2 garlic cloves, cut into strips
1 tbsp soy sauce
a little oil
1 (450g / 1lb) red mullet, fully gutted
1 bunch fresh coriander
chilli peppers and cucumber to decorate

Preparation

Mix the beanshoots, ginger, garlic and soy sauce together and stuff the mixture inside the cavity of the fish. Brush a large sheet of foil with oil, place the stuffed mullet in the centre and scatter half the coriander leaves over. Wrap the fish in a tight foil parcel and place on a baking sheet.

Final cooking and serving

Set the oven at 200°C/400°F/gas 6.

Bake the fish for 20 minutes. Open the parcel and transfer the mullet on to a serving dish. Pour the cooking juices over and garnish with the remaining coriander leaves, chilli peppers and cucumber.

PINEAPPLE DELIGHT WITH LYCHEE FLOWERS

This recipe is not in the least authentic Chinese, or Turkish for that matter! It does, however, look oriental and will make the perfect ending to your banquet.

🕐 25 minutes
Serves 6

1 large pineapple
225g / 8oz Turkish delight
450g / 1lb fresh lychees

Cut the pineapple lengthways into six, including the prickly top. Scoop the flesh out of each section of skin, discard the core and chop the rest into small chunks. Cut the Turkish delight into similar-sized pieces, mix these with the pineapple flesh and re-fill the six sections of skin.

Using a paring knife, score the skin of the lychees into four quarter sections without cutting the fruit inside. Peel back the four 'petals' of skin to make a flower. Arrange the pineapple sections on a round dish with a cluster of lychee flowers in the centre.

Cut the pineapple into six as shown.

Score the lychees and fold back the 'petals'.

Supper on the Cheap

Christmas has had the usual effect of bankrupting us all but you should refuse to let that halt your life of entertaining. Soup and a scone followed by a few rounds of whist will suffice perfectly. Tell your friends to provide a bottle of plonk.

PHEASANT POACHER'S SOUP

ANCHOVY AND ONION SCONES

CHICKEN LIVER AND CROUTON SALAD

AUBERGINE AND COURGETTE LASAGNE

TARTE TATIN

PHEASANT POACHER'S SOUP

And I have to say not a very successful poacher. Only one pheasant and six people to feed off it.

🕐 5 hours on and off, including cooking
Serves 6

25g / 1oz lard
1 large pheasant
6 bacon rashers
1 onion, chopped
2 old carrots, chopped
50g / 2oz plain flour
1.75 litres / 3 pints cold water
75ml / 3 fl oz medium sherry
1 tbsp brown sugar
1 tbsp lemon juice
100g / 4oz pearl barley
salt and freshly ground black pepper
fresh chervil leaves

Set the oven at 220°C/425°F/gas 7.

Put the lard and pheasant in a roasting tin. Lay the bacon rashers over the bird and roast in the oven for 45 minutes.

Once out of the oven cool enough to handle, remove the bacon, chop it into small pieces and keep to one side. Lift the pheasant out of the tin and carefully scrape all the dripping into a large saucepan. Carve the flesh off the bird, save the bones and cut the meat into small strips. Add the meat to the bacon.

Heat the saucepan of dripping and cook the pheasant bones, giblets, onion and carrots. Brown this mixture for a good 10 minutes, stirring occasionally. Now stir in the flour and cook for a further 3–4 minutes until it is well browned but not burnt. Add all the water. Stir well, then leave on a low heat to simmer for 1½–2 hours.

Sieve the mixture to remove the bones and vegetables, then return the liquid to a clean saucepan. Add the sherry, brown sugar, lemon juice, pearl barley, salt and pepper, and cook for a further 40 minutes, stirring occasionally. Finally, add the pheasant meat and bacon.

Serve the soup with a sprinkling of chervil leaves.

ANCHOVY AND ONION SCONES

I am no great baker but there is nothing easier than home-made scones and my guests are always terribly impressed. They are also a perfect example of a baker's dozen; this recipe is intended to make thirteen – the first one definitely has the cook's name on it.

🕐 20 minutes, plus 15 minutes in the oven
Makes 13

1 small onion, finely chopped
a little margarine for cooking
225g / 8oz plain flour
½ tsp salt
½ tsp bicarbonate of soda
25g / 1oz butter
6 anchovy fillets, finely chopped (optional)
150ml / ¼ pint milk
1 tsp cream of tartar

Set the oven at 200°C/400°F/gas 6.

Fry the onion in the margarine until soft, then leave on one side to cool. Mix the flour, salt, bicarbonate of soda and butter together in a bowl and then mix in the cold onion and the anchovy. Mix the milk and cream of tartar together, add this to the other ingredients and knead them all together.

Turn the dough on to a floured surface and pat it down flat to a thickness of about 2.5cm/1 inch. Using a 5-cm/2-inch pastry cutter, cut out rounds, then knead the remainder together and cut out again. Place the rounds on an oiled baking sheet and bake for 15 minutes.

CHICKEN LIVER AND CROUTON SALAD

I should really call this garlic salad but then everyone would be put off. It is, however, a formula for filling your home with the wonderful wafting smells of garlic and then guzzling it to your heart's content.

🕐 20 minutes
Serves 6

½ punnet lamb's tongue salad
1 radicchio leaf
1 small oak leaf lettuce
4 tbsp oil
1 garlic clove, crushed
4 thick slices of bread, cut into squares
225g / 8oz chicken livers, chopped
another 2 garlic cloves, finely chopped
salt and freshly ground black pepper
2 tbsp sherry vinegar
2 tsp soft brown sugar
1 more garlic clove, crushed

Tear the lamb's tongue salad, radicchio and oak leaf lettuce into tufts and arrange on a serving dish. Heat the oil in a pan, add the first clove of crushed garlic and fry the bread to a golden colour. Drain on kitchen paper towels and keep warm.

Now, cook the chicken livers in the pan together with the finely chopped garlic and plenty of salt and pepper. Toss in the pan for

about 5 minutes until fully cooked; then, using a slotted spoon, arrange the livers on top of the salad. Return the pan to the heat, add the vinegar, sugar and the last crushed garlic clove. Cook for a few moments and spoon over the salad. Scatter croûtons on the top and serve.

Careful whom you kiss later!

AUBERGINE AND COURGETTE LASAGNE

A perfect dish to keep in the freezer, ready to produce a wholesome, tasty meal on a day when you have no time at all. It also makes a delicious dinner party starter served in ramekins.

🕐 45 minutes, plus 20 minutes in the oven
Serves 6

2 tbsp oil
1 onion, chopped
1 aubergine, diced
450g / 1lb courgettes, sliced
1 (400g / 14oz) can tomatoes
75ml / 3 fl oz red wine (water would do)
2 tbsp tomato purée
1 garlic clove, crushed
salt and freshly ground black pepper
1 tsp dried mixed herbs
175g / 6oz sheet pasta
50g / 2oz margarine
50g / 2oz plain flour
600ml / 1 pint milk
75g / 3oz Cheddar cheese, grated

Preparation
Heat the oil in a pan and cook the onion until soft. Add the aubergine and toss in the pan for 2 minutes; the dice will absorb the oil quickly and then scorch slightly. Now

115

add the courgette, tomato, red wine, tomato purée and garlic. Bring to the boil and simmer for 20 minutes, stirring occasionally. Season with salt, pepper and dried herbs.

Transfer the mixture to an ovenproof dish and spread it out flat. Cover with a complete layer of pasta sheets.

Melt the margarine in a clean pan, stir in the flour and cook for 1 minute. Remove from the heat and stir in the milk, a little at a time. Return to the heat, bring to the boil, add the grated cheese and season. Pour the cheese mixture over the pasta. The dish can now be allowed to cool until needed.

Final cooking and serving
Set the oven at 200°C/400°F/gas 6.

Bake the lasagne for 20 minutes until golden brown on top. Serve with a green salad.

TARTE TATIN

An upside-down caramel and apple flan named after some famous French cook whom I try not to think about. I only get jealous.

🕐 45 minutes, plus 40 minutes in the oven
Serves 6

150g / 5oz caster sugar
100g / 4oz butter
3 Bramley apples, peeled, cored and sliced
450g / 1lb rich shortcrust pastry (page 95)

Set the oven at 200°C/400°F/gas 6 and find a suitable solid-bottomed 20-cm/8-inch flan tin.

Put the sugar and butter together in a pan and melt over a low heat. Stirring

occasionally, allow the sugar first to melt, then slowly turn to a rich dark caramel. Pour the caramel into the base of the tin. Immediately, arrange a bottom layer of apple slices in the caramel and then pack all the remaining apple on top.

Roll out the pastry to a slightly larger circle than the tin. Place this over the apple and tuck the edge down firmly inside the tin.

Bake for 40 minutes, then allow to cool slightly before turning out on to a serving dish. The tart can be served right away or re-heated later. Lashings of whipped cream or crème fraîche are a must to go with it.

Pour the caramel into the flan tin.

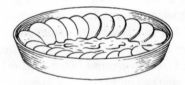

Arrange a layer of apple slices in the caramel and pack the remaining slices on top.

Cover with pastry, tucking the edge inside the tin.

Valentine's Seduction

Valentine's Day is a curious concept. It can be considered either wildly romantic or rather corny and passé. I remember sending my first-ever Valentine card when I considered myself to be a budding young artist. Alas, when the recipient received my masterpiece, the paint (not quite dry) had firmly stuck to the envelope. The romance was off.

Romantic food is another thing altogether and I have created a special Valentine's menu for two. You may find it romantic, seductive or just amusing but, whichever, at least you won't have to put it in an envelope.

BAKED OYSTERS AND ARTICHOKES
IN CHAMPAGNE SAUCE

CHICKEN WITH PASSION-FRUIT AND CASHEW NUTS
IN A VALENTINE CROUSTADE
FRESH ASPARAGUS

CHOCOLATE AND GRAND MARNIER FONDUE

BAKED OYSTERS AND ARTICHOKES IN CHAMPAGNE SAUCE

Oysters are the ultimate, sophisticated aphrodisiac and a must for a truly successful Valentine's supper. They are traditionally eaten raw with a little lemon juice but this is not to everyone's taste. In this recipe the oysters are lightly baked and served in their shells alongside a crisp, leafy salad.

🕐 30 minutes, plus 5 minutes in the oven
Serves 2

6 fresh oysters
1 (225g / 8oz) can artichoke hearts

Sauce
125ml / 4 fl oz champagne or white wine
2 shallots, finely chopped
1 tbsp lemon vinegar
1 tsp caster sugar
salt and freshly ground black pepper
2 tbsp double cream
1 egg yolk

Salad
50g / 2oz lamb's tongue salad
1 small piece lollo rosso lettuce
1 Little Gem lettuce
fresh basil leaves (if available)
olive oil
lemon juice
salt and freshly ground black pepper

Preparation
Begin by opening the oysters without stabbing yourself – beware! Wrap a thick cloth around one hand and grip the oyster in it. Insert a short, pointed knife into the join of the two shells. Twist the knife and prise open. Now free the oyster from the shell, keep the lid on one side and leave the flesh in the bottom half.

Slice the artichoke hearts and place two or three slices in each shell with the oyster. Place the shells in a baking tin ready to cook at the last minute.

To prepare the sauce, simmer the champagne or white wine, shallots, vinegar and sugar for about 5 minutes. Season well. Mix the cream and egg yolk together and stir this into the liquid. Cook for a few moments until the sauce thickens but be careful not to let it boil. Remove from the heat and spoon over the oysters and artichokes. Replace the lids on the shells.

Tear the salad leaves into small tufts and dress lightly with olive oil, lemon juice, salt and pepper. Toss the salad and arrange in the centre of a 'romantic' serving platter.

Final cooking and serving
Set the oven at 180°C/350°F/gas 4.

Just before serving, bake the oysters for 5 minutes. Arrange them around the salad and serve.

CHICKEN WITH PASSION-FRUIT AND CASHEW NUTS IN A VALENTINE CROUSTADE

Passion-fruit is another perfect ingredient for a Valentine's recipe. This dish comprises individual heart-shaped pastry cases (*croustade* is a fancy name for a big *vol-au-vent*), filled with chicken and cashew nuts and finished with tangy passion-fruit seeds.

🕐 50 minutes, plus 10 minutes in the oven
Serves 2

100g / 4oz frozen puff pastry, thawed
egg wash (whole egg and salt mixed)

Filling

25g / 1oz margarine
225g / 8oz chicken breasts, cut into small strips
50g / 2oz cashew nuts
25g / 1oz plain flour
300ml / ½ pint stock
1 garlic clove, crushed
salt and freshly ground black pepper
1 passion-fruit, scooped out of the shell
chopped parsley

Preparation
Set the oven at 200°C/400°F/gas 6.

Roll out the pastry to an even oblong about 6mm/¼ inch thick. To the best of your ability, cut out two heart shapes! With the tip of the knife, score an inner heart on the pastry without cutting right through, leaving a border of about 1cm/½ inch. Brush the pastry with egg wash and place on an oiled baking sheet. Place a wire rack over the top of the hearts to ensure the pastry rises evenly. Bake for 10 minutes.

When the pastry is cooked to a golden-brown, re-trace the inner cut and remove the inside lid; scoop out the loose pastry from the inside.

Melt the margarine in a pan and fry the strips of chicken lightly but until fully cooked. Add the cashew nuts, then scoop out the chicken and nuts with a slotted spoon. Stir the flour into the pan; cook for 1 minute, then add the stock gradually, stirring continuously. Add the garlic and season with salt and pepper; finally, add the passion-fruit seeds and leave to one side.

Final cooking and serving
Set the oven at 180°C/350°F/gas 4.

Just before serving, fill each pastry heart with chicken and cashew nuts and place in the oven for 5 minutes. Re-heat the sauce on the hob. Place the hearts on individual plates, spoon some sauce and passion-fruit over the chicken and add more on the plate alongside. Sprinkle chopped parsley on to the hearts and serve.

The perfect accompaniment would be fresh asparagus. Although out of season, imported asparagus should be available and well worth the extravagance.

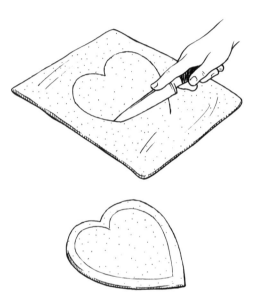

Cut out two heart shapes and then score each as shown.

Chocolate and Grand Marnier Fondue

We have enhanced desire with oysters, we have inscribed our love in a heart-shaped croustade – now a wickedly rich fondue shared by the fire has to be the perfect seduction.

🕐 25 minutes
Serves 2

225g / 8oz bitter or plain chocolate
300ml / ½ pint cold water
100g / 4oz granulated sugar
4 tbsp Grand Marnier
grated zest of 1 orange

Fruits
2 kiwi fruits, peeled and sliced
a few strawberries
a few apricots, halved, stoned and sliced
2 dessert pears, peeled and sliced

Break the chocolate into small pieces and put in a saucepan with the water. Melt the chocolate over a low heat. Stir the mixture and, when smooth, add the sugar. Bring to the boil and simmer until the fondue reduces and thickens (about 10 minutes). Add a good slurp of Grand Marnier (I have been more precise above) and the grated orange zest. Remove from the heat until required.

Arrange the prepared fruits in a thoroughly artistic way (that was helpful), re-heat the fondue and then, side-by-side, you and your Valentine will dip pieces of fruit into the hot chocolate while gazing into each other's eyes.

In Conclusion –
Clearing Up

After all that lovely food, what a terrible subject to finish this book on – but, let's face it, at the end of every party lies the clearing up. There is a choice of two evils: do you tackle the mess at 2AM when the last guest has finally staggered home? Or do you face it in the morning when your hangover and the washing-up can compete as reasons to feel sorry for yourself. Alas, I have no miracle solutions this time.

There follow the traditional postmortems about who was ignored and who was monopolized. Why did no-one eat more pud and what's to be done about the stain on the sideboard? Inevitably a sense of anti-climax.

All I can suggest is a nice cup of tea and some positive thinking while you work. After all, it did go well and was great fun. But then what? Why of course, plan the next party!

LIST OF MENUS

ENTERTAINING IN
THE SPRING

ENTERTAINING IN THE SUMMER

ENTERTAINING IN
THE AUTUMN

ENTERTAINING IN THE WINTER

INDEX